Greatness is a Shadow

How to Transform Your Life and Walk in Your Purpose

BARRY JOHNSON

CJ LEGACY PUBLISHING INC. |

Published by CJ Legacy Publishing Inc.

DEDICATIONS

This book is written and dedicated to my children, May each of them realize and be conscious of their God-given Greatness and soar . . .

This book is also written and dedicated to my Mother, Mary S. Fitzgerald. She realized both of our God-given Greatness, she poured into me so that I could one day soar...

This book is written and dedicated to every person that has either hurt me, or helped me, along the way;

For those who hurt me, I thank you for preparing me for what God had for me; because in that hurt, you helped me find my strength and ability to overcome...

For those who did their best to help me, I thank you for protecting me, praying for me, and providing for me, and shielding me from those people and those things that would hurt me.

TRIBUTE

To my wife, Nedra Johnson…who always leaves me totally
BREATHLESS;

Thank you.

You build me up.

You speak life and possibility into my soul and into my
being.

You make me want to be better; then, you make me better.

You balance me.

You strengthen me.

You encourage me.

You teach me.

You complete me and make me whole.

Your presence, aura and spirit is evidence that God lives
within all of us. When I walk with you, I get to walk with
God. How blessed I am to have heaven here on earth.

I am blessed to have met and married my soul mate and my
best friend.

This book would not have been possible, nor would the
Greatness that is in me, were it not for you, helping me,
teaching me and seeing the God in me.

I love you.

"Despise not the day of small beginnings"

Zechariah 4:10

I am indebted to the mercy and favor of God for all He has done and all he continues to do; for He has given me a life of experiences that made this book possible.

Preface

"My life is my message"
—Mahatma Gandhi

For those who know me, and my life's journey, have seen me traverse through times both good and bad, with highs and lows, with wealth and without, in happiness and sorrow, in love and in loneliness. I have lived my life unapologetically.

At times, I have lived with unyielding effort, relentless commitment and drive. At other times, I have lived foolishly and childishly; without thought: haste! That haste was too often fueled or created by emotional responses of either insecurity, fear, doubt, ignorance, jealousy, desperation or impatience. At times, it was created or fueled by all of these at once.

And so, *Life for me*, in the soulful words of the immortal and legendary Harlem Renaissance bard Langston Hughes, *ain't been no crystal stair*. It's had some tacks in it and splinters, and boards torn up, and places, with no carpet on the floor. Bare.

As I began to put pen to paper to write this book, I reflected on where I have been, and how I got here. I wanted this book to be vulnerably transparent in order that it resonate with people on so many levels. Transparency, for me, also meant an opportunity to "let go." Let go of the anger, let go of the fear, let go of the resentment, let go of the pain, let go of the shame and let go of all the ghosts and the experiences, and the disappointments that I have held onto throughout my life and that I have allowed to define me. I wanted all these experiences to finally be out of my head and out of my heart.

Then, I suddenly realized that my story is probably not so different from the stories and experiences of so many others. In fact, my story is probably not so different than your own. Although the facts and circumstances will certainly change depending on who you are and where you come from, most of us can still probably agree that life consists of and requires constant growth and adaptation.

PREFACE

Despite any of our individual circumstances, we have all had to climb our way up and out of some difficult times and situations. We have all had, at some point, to reach deeper and climb higher in order to reach safe harbors, find secure landings, turn some sharp corners and go into some really dark places with no light in sight. These dark places are filled with conditions, circumstances, uncertainties and unknowns and we usually have no idea what is going to happen to us or where we might end up.

The dark places are where we obviously always "seem" to lack any "real" illumination. It's the dark places where our hope is not so abundant. In these dark places, is where we tend to be led more by fear rather than by faith. It is in these darkest places where we begin to pray and ask the heavenly and omnipotent God for answers to help shed light. Ironically, those answers can be found in the God that exist within each of us. It is in these darkest places where our faith, is the very light that would, or could, illuminate our way.

People say you never know quite how strong you really are, until times get so bad that strength must be found, because strength is all you have left.

As I previously proffered, all of us share some commonalities and similarities of dark moments and uncertainty and fear in our individual life stories. You and I both know what we have been through. Yet, through it all, we are both still here. This, to me, is evidence that God is not through with either of us yet.

God restores us every day as we rest. Then, He calls us every day to awaken and He gives us a New Day. He calls us with His light, and towards His promise. Each new day, He grants us another opportunity to walk in our purpose, realize our possibilities and live up to our fullest potential. I believe that where our "possibility" and "potential" end, is where our death begins.

When we celebrate the new born life of a child, we are celebrating the creation and birth of a new possibility. We are celebrating the creation and birth of a gift from God. God's gift is full of potential, full of possibility, full of God's promise. But also with this gift, none of us have any idea, where this new life will go, or what this child will do or become, yet we celebrate it still. The birth of a new child is shrouded in uncertainty and unknowns, yet we celebrate it still.

Why then, is it that when we deal with unknowns, uncertainties and darkness in our own lives, that we treat it so differently? Why in our own lives when we are faced with hardship, uncertainty and darkness our hope is not so abundant? But then, in the life of a new child, a gift from God, we deal with the very same uncertainty and unknowns for that child's life from a place of abundant hope, faith and belief in His power and His grace.

What causes us to treat the same type of uncertainties and unknowns to be handled in such different ways? In our own lives the uncertain and unknown times are viewed from a place of fear and darkness and a lack of illumination while in the life of a new child, the uncertain and unknown times are viewed from a place of hope, faith, and God's light.

Greatness is a Shadow celebrates and exalts the possibility and potential of God's promise in YOU. The fact that you have chosen to read this book, tells me all I need to know about you. I know, and you know, there is "something" inside you. Inside you, is something that beckons you, that pushes you to get up, to press through, and to strive toward what to many seems insurmountable and unreachable. That "something" I call Greatness.

Your story does not end there, because along with that Greatness, something else lives inside you called Purpose. So despite your circumstance, despite your hardship, despite your pain, despite your fear, despite the darkness, despite it all, God is in you and therefore, Greatness is in you.

And so yes, this book is a piece of my story, but in so many ways, I am sure it will prove itself to be just as much a piece of your own story. You will come to realize throughout this book, that neither condition, nor circumstance means anything to either of us anymore. From here on, you and I can have more, do more, be more. You and I can walk in our God-given purpose and carry out more than we ever dreamed imaginable or attainable. We can do better and we can be greater. Your greatness may not look, nor feel, nor sound like mine, nor maybe even the next person's, and that's okay, because your Greatness is yours. We may not be equal in size, nor equal in weight, nor equal in material possessions but we are all equal in what God has created us to be. Your crystal stair is what God uniquely created and gave unto you. Greatness demands you go for "it", whatever "it" is, and Greatness demands you do "it" no matter what.

So, clearly then, this book is not about me. Instead, it's a story about you. It is a story about Greatness.

A word of admonition; life has made clear that attaining "it" or attaining Greatness, feels satisfying and fulfilling, but that feeling lasts but for only a moment. Lord knows I live for those moments. The thing about Greatness is that "it" is a continually moving target. Why? Because God has no limits, no boundaries, and He is Omnipotent. The "Next Level" always exist. Another dimension is always possible. Higher iterations of your life and your Greatness will continue to manifest themselves in your life and in the lives of the people in which you surround yourself. Possibility and potential is never a final destination, nor could it ever be. Your "purpose" in living is inextricably tied to God's continued grace and giving. Just as His giving never stops and His grace never ends, so how could then ever the possibility and potential in you ever reach its bound. There is always a greater iteration of wherever you are currently. Where most of us see ourselves as a Human Being, God created us to be a Human Becoming. Accordingly, "it" changes as you change. Growth rarely happens at the same moment "it" is realized, but rather your growth happens AS "it" happens. So "it" happens along the journey; "it" happens in the process. Your Greatness happens in your being as you are becoming.

As you grow, as you learn, as you love, as you hurt, as you succeed, as you win, as you fail and as you lose, your "it" will evolve as you evolve. Inevitably, through it all, greatness emerges. Success in striving toward greatness, begets success of even greater greatness.

Interestingly, at the center of these quests or pursuits are always going to be specific hardships, burdens and pain that must be overcome. The pain or the "process" inevitably makes you better, stronger, more resilient, but scarred nonetheless. Albeit these scars are mere beauty marks that elucidate your greatness and evidence your journey.

It is in recognition of the process, that this book will seek to reveal your Greatness. It is in the process that a level of consciousness and acuity must be awakened and realized. This consciousness must be specific and purposeful and intentional. This consciousness requires effort. The thing about effort and consciousness is that it is easy to do, and even easier not to do.

Throughout this book you will inevitably come to your own conclusions about what Greatness means and how Greatness can be found in all of us. As for me, my journey toward Greatness started out in a small southern furniture manufacturing town called High Point, North Carolina.

Chapter 1

The Meaning Behind the Metaphor

"Man was designed for accomplishment, engineered for success, and endowed with the seeds of greatness."

—Zig Ziglar

As you are called, so shall be your commitment. My prayer is that this book creates a newly found consciousness for some, and a heightened consciousness for others, that will encourage, equip and enable you to walk in your purpose, transform your life and cast your shadow of greatness upon the universe. But, what exactly does it mean to "cast your shadow of greatness?"

THE SHADOW CONCEPT

A shadow is a dark area or shape that is produced when something comes in between a ray of light and a surface. If a light is shining and you walk in front of that light, you will cast a shadow onto whatever is around you. Your shadow might be cast on the ground or on the wall or it might be cast behind you, in front of you, or beside you.

Even now, as you are reading or listening to this book, you undoubtedly are casting a shadow. And although you may not see your shadow right now, you unconsciously know that it is there.

Interestingly, most of us are highly unlikely to even see, notice or realize our shadow until we "decide" or choose to "consciously" look for it. When was the last time you "decided" or "chose" to purposefully and specifically look for your shadow? And why would you? What result would that seemingly meaningless effort even produce?

Every day, each and every one of us, at some point catches a glimpse of our own shadow, but rarely do we even acknowledge its presence. Certainly, we never set out with the specific intention to find our shadow, nor focus on it. When we do see our shadow, we are subtly and unconsciously reminded that it is there. Ironically though, our shadow is cast even when we are not aware, nor conscious of its presence.

Now, compare that reality to the vast amount of people who walk around their entire lives not realizing their power, their purpose, their passion and without a clue on how to even tap into their greatness. Just like with the shadow, they make no effort to see it, nor effort to live it, nor any effort to exalt it.

The level of effort to choose or decide to consciously look for your shadow is the same level of effort it takes to consciously walk in your purpose and step into your greatness. Greatness, like a shadow, is in all of us, but in order for any of us to see it, or live it, or walk in it, we must put forth a conscious and intentional effort. And not some casual effort either, but rather a purposeful, intentional, specific and conscious effort. But effort, nonetheless.

Greatness is in all of us.

THE GREATNESS CONCEPT

I have come to realize that people, in general, refer to greatness all the time in their day to day conversations about other people, places or things. Rarely do we think of ourselves in terms of our own capacity for greatness or potential.

Even the definition of greatness is elusive. If you ask your ten closest friends how they would define greatness, I imagine you will get ten different answers. How then, could it even be possible that we all have greatness within us, yet we do not readily understand what greatness is or how to define it. If that reality seems implausible, then maybe you should ask yourself a different question.

Like greatness, the definition of purpose is also elusive. If you ask your ten closest friends how they would define purpose, I imagine you would also get ten different answers.

Do you believe that every person has a purpose in or for their life? Do you believe that God bestowed purpose to some, and not to others? Or maybe it is that, those you think do not have any purpose for their life, just have not figured out how to recognize it, nor tap into it. If so, how then would you help them define purpose, and more specifically their purpose or even your own purpose for your life, and how would you or they recognize that purpose so both of you could act upon it.

Like purpose, greatness is in all of us, yet we can't even agree on a definition or understanding of what greatness even means.

Google defines greatness, like this:

great·ness: 'grātnəs/ noun: the quality of being great, distinguished, or eminent.

synonyms: eminence, distinction, illustriousness, repute, high standing; importance, significance; celebrity, fame, prominence, renown, genius, prowess, talent, expertise, mastery, artistry, virtuosity, skill, proficiency; flair, finesse; caliber, distinction

MEANING BEHIND THE METAPHOR

Nothing in Google's definition gives us any real clarity on understanding the meaning of greatness. Wikipedia does not offer much help or clarity either. Wikipedia defines Greatness as:

"a concept of a state of superiority affecting a person or object. Greatness can also be referred to individuals who possess a natural ability to be better than all others. The concept carries the implication that the particular person or object, when compared to others of a similar type, has clear advantage over others. As a descriptive term it is most often applied to a person or their work, and may be qualified or unqualified."

The online Urban Dictionary gives us a little more context for greatness to work with:

"greatness is an acquisition of status by the people who have contributed to an organization, group, or purpose that is greater than themselves. It is defined by the deeds of people that make this world a better place. To provide a purpose to those who have no purpose, and to sustain it, mitigate it from damage, and praise it in any way they can, while still maintaining their own dignity and greatness."

So, arguably, if we don't even have a consensus or baseline standard of a starting point for understanding, recognizing, defining and conceptualizing greatness, how then do we even measure or attempt to achieve our own capacity for greatness?

In writing *Greatness is a Shadow*, God gave me my own definition of greatness in short form and in long form. I offer them both to you:

Greatness in Short Form

Greatness (verb): Living an authentic life where you are constantly becoming and trying to be the absolute best version of yourself in everything you do and in every place you show up.

Greatness in Long Form

Greatness (verb): Greatness is the culmination of your conscious, intentional, specific, purposeful decisions and actions in choosing to live your life in such a manner where you constantly compete against yourself to become better than you were yesterday; to have more, do more, be more, inspire more, help more, give more, serve more, and love more in how you approach everything, and how you interact with everybody. Greatness means recognition, consciousness and acquiescence of your gifts, talents and abilities, and respecting them in such a way that you choose to maximize them and utilize them to the fullest, in everything you do, while holding nothing back.

MEANING BEHIND THE METAPHOR

Here is what's so powerful about the greatness that each of us possesses: just like your shadow, when greatness shows up, sometimes you don't even see it; because that "thing" we are seemingly destined for, that "thing" we're so great at, or that "thing" that we seem to do just so easily, we're not paying any attention to, but everyone else seems to make such a big deal about. You don't acknowledge it because whatever that thing is for you, "it" comes so naturally, that to you, "its" just there. Just like with our shadow, we take it for granted because we know that it's just there. Call it talent! Call it a gift! Call it anointing! Call it blessed! Call it what you want, but with everyone you meet and with everything you do, "it" just keeps showing up naturally because it is part of you.

But, unfortunately, just because you have "it", does not mean you are conscious of it. And because you are unconscious of it, then you, nor the people you love, nor the things that matter, nor the circumstances around you ever benefit from it, nor are positively affected by it. So rather than walking in your greatness, many of us instead choose to walk in mediocrity. Rather than experiencing greatness, we instead choose to be the product of whatever our circumstances have dealt us.

Then again, there are also those of us who are conscious of "it", but we don't allow ourselves to focus on it, nor maximize it, nor use that gift, that blessing, that talent, that anointing, that thing. But why? Why can't we focus on it? The reason we just can't focus on it is because of the stories we tell ourselves and that others have told us about ourselves. Our experiences, our failures, our doubts, and our concerns about what other people may say or think place limits upon our ability to reach our greatness. You know those stories that give us arguably, and defensively VALID circumstances and justifications that we hold on to and have now convinced ourselves to settle for (also known as our excuses that we call reasons, hardships, beliefs, fears, doubts, finances, or lack of time, support, and resources you do not have) that consume every part of you and all of you; limiting beliefs.

THE "GREATNESS IS A SHADOW" CONCEPT

In order to cast a shadow, or to cast your greatness, you must place yourself in between a "ray of light" and some person or object. In 1 John 1:5 we find "God is light." The fact that God is light sets up a concomitant phenomena for your shadow and your Greatness to be cast upon your circumstances, as well as objects and people that come into your presence.

Every person can cast a shadow of greatness.

THE LIGHT WITHIN

Not only do you have the external omnipresence of God as your ray of light all around you, but you also have an internal presence of God that illuminates within you. If you and I can get to a place of consciousness of that internal light within, then we will be able to "acknowledge" the presence of God that abides in each of us. This light is a spiritual light house that is inside you, all around you and serves as your beacon for possibility. People can sense, and the universe knows when you are radiating the light of God inside you. As His light radiates within you, shadows of your potential and your unique greatness are cast all around you. It is in that shadow you cast, that you can rest, have peace, and shelter from any stress and be your absolute best self and most authentic self. In order for you to manifest power from the internal light you have within you, the universe will unapologetically require a spirit of gratitude.

GRATEFULNESS IS A CONDITION PRECEDENT TO GREATNESS

Gratefulness or gratitude is the precursor to greatness. Gratefulness is a condition precedent to greatness. Your greatness will show up and manifests itself in everything you do and be felt by everyone around you where "gratefulness" genuinely exists.

We show our gratefulness and express or display gratitude or appreciation to God for his ray of light that illuminates inside us by how we "consciously" "decide" and choose to live our lives on a day to day basis. Gratefulness shows in how you approach everything, and how you deal with everyone. Gratefulness is evidenced by your intentional, specific and purposeful actions of compounding improvement in the gifts, blessings, anointing, talents and skill and, that "it", that God gave uniquely to you. To whom much is given, much is expected. Gratefulness will fuel you to grow those talents and create a foundation of living based upon them. Gratefulness rejects merely being and chooses becoming.

So, what would happen then, if you knew that greatness was inside you the same way you know you have a shadow?

And what would happen if every time you did anything at all, you did it with an intentional, specific and purposeful **step** in the direction of your gifts and your greatness and thereby revealed your gratefulness.

If greatness meant getting up an hour earlier to put in calls to potential clients or business partners to accomplish your goal. If greatness meant healthier, mindful alternative choices, about what you're going to eat that day, to accomplish your fitness and weight goal.

MEANING BEHIND THE METAPHOR

Greatness might mean that you will start going for a walk or run before you go to bed at night to accomplish your fitness goals. It might mean turning off your smart phones or digital devices, so you can spend actively engaged time with your children or the people you love. Every **step** in the direction of your greatness puts you in oneness with the purpose for which you were created. Creating small victories that you will achieve every day is what I want to help you celebrate. I want you to have daily victories that are achievable and realistic.

In *Greatness is a Shadow: Transform Your Life and Walk in Your Purpose*, I want to encourage you to capitalize on every one of those singular and isolated moments. Those moments where "choices" are made. Choices that make incremental and marginal progress in you and who you are becoming and that allow you to be the best and most authentic version of you. Choices which have a compound effect in reaching your greatness and holding nothing back. Les Brown would say "Live full and die empty". Greatness is what happens when you're completely emptied.

> *"I think anybody who's great is somebody who just doesn't give up. In the face of adversity they don't give up. It also comes down to character. They wanna be successful, but at the same time success has a greater meaning. It's not just*

financial; it's in relationships, in life. It's this well balanced, well rounded life."

Throughout the pages of *Greatness Is a Shadow: Transform Your Life and Walk in Your Purpose*, you will acquire a heightened awareness or consciousness of your shadow and embrace your God-given greatness.

As you continue to read, you will notice that on some key principles, the tone of my delivery may seem to escalate, and I may even use an occasional expletive, but I ask that you please be less concerned about the emphatic and oft times passionate language and more concerned about the message.

Life is short, and greatness is calling you. This book is not intended to be a "feel good" placid inspirational or motivational guide. This is an up-close-and-personal, let's-get-it-done PLEA for you to wake up, step up and walk in your purpose because your best self, your family, your children, your significant other, your community and your Creator are all waiting for you. God, Himself, ordained and installed purpose IN YOU since you were born and that purpose is YOURS and cannot be fulfilled by anyone else's life but YOURS.

So yes, I am going to push you toward your greatness. Why? Because greatness is in you! It's always been in you, just like your shadow has always been with you. You have to put forth effort to see it, to recognize and walk in the power that emanates from it; then to actualize it, operate in it, and desire it with a passion in knowing that your God-given purpose resides in it.

I'm going to stretch you in ways that may be a little uncomfortable and I want to make you uncomfortable. I want to cause you to grow, and to become. I want to be an encourager who shows tough love, but I want you to understand that there is an unconditional love that motivates me. It is in that love, then, I can offer myself to you – in full transparency – throughout this journey.

Understand that what I share throughout this book comes from the personal and professional experiences, failures and successes of my own life. These experiences have at times caused me to get knocked flat on my back. But as I have been down, with my head bloody, yet still unbowed, I choose to keep my eyes on Him. I don't listen to what they say about me, good or bad. I don't worry about what they think about me, good or bad. As I focus on Him, I stay connected to Him. I stay in His ray of light, and I am able to tap into that internal light, which gives me my strength. It is in that strength that the Next Level is realized.

Greatness is a Shadow is a transformative book. Greatness is a Shadow is about who you are becoming, rather than who you are being. Greatness is a Shadow will transform the relationships you have with other people and the relationship you will have with yourself. Imagine a next level in your mind, body and being where the version of you that shows up is the best version of you possible. Now imagine living every area of your life as that expanded version of yourself. Imagine a version of you that is so constantly powerful, conscious and aware, that you have options about how you will consciously show up in response to life, people and circumstances.

THE PROCESS REQUIRES CONSCIOUSNESS

Writing *Greatness is a Shadow* allowed me to have honest self-reflection and deep introspection. I have come to recognize the greatest achievement in my life has not **been becoming "successful."** Instead, it has been the **successful "Process" of becoming**. The process is always where the magic happens. Often times, unfortunately, for so many people the process is cut short because they do not have the mindset or mental fortitude to grow through the process.

But what, exactly, is this "process" and how does one grow through it? Throughout this Introduction, you have seen that I continually highlight "consciousness" or awareness or acuity and acknowledgement. Why? Because for me, the process has meant continually learning and continually mastering the "discipline of consciousness."

MEANING BEHIND THE METAPHOR

Consciousness, I believe, is a learned behavior. It is a discipline, a mindset. The discipline of consciousness or awareness or acuity comes through mental conditioning which leads to mental endurance.

Like in sports for example, an athlete's level of physical endurance stems directly from the amount of physical conditioning the athlete has been through. That conditioning comes through constant, consistent and regular practice. Championships are not won during the championship game. Instead, Championships are won during the day after day processes and practices that happen all season leading up to the championship game. It is that constant, consistent and regular day to day practice that creates preparation and readiness in an athlete for that championship game.

Consciousness, too, comes through a constant, consistent and regular process. You can't hit a button and say, ok, now I'm conscious. The consciousness I speak of is not only awareness and acuity, but its also acknowledgement, acceptance and acquiescence, and most importantly, persistence in your decision to be conscious. It means consistency in your commitment with commitment to consistency.

I do not profess to have succeeded at all of the things I would like to, nor those that I need to. Instead what I do claim, is that I am a human becoming, not just a human being. Every day, I awaken with the specific, intentional and purposeful goal of embodying my best self. I choose to live boldly, unapologetically, majestically and with expectancy for me and my queen. My goal is that Nedra and I can grow together, build together and become everything we possibly can, individually and as a couple.

Every day, we employ, encourage and hold one another accountable so that we are constantly defining and reshaping our beliefs, perceptions, and mindset in such a manner that we cannot only impact our own lives and the lives of our children, but that we might transform lives of those around us. We consciously give ourselves permission every day to expand in some way, so that we might exalt one another, while exalting the word of God.

Mental endurance is the product of mental conditioning of consciousness, and it produces a "can do", "must do", "will do", "never quit" attitude, and an undeniable, unshakable and impenetrable belief and confidence in one's self that always propels people who possess it to the Next Level – This consciousness is manifested in one's recognition of having been equipped with a **God-ordained purpose** for your own life that **no one else** has other than you.

Indeed, as we begin to jump into the first chapter of *Greatness is a Shadow*, please understand I am a survivor. Me being a survivor only exists because God is a restorer and a redeemer. I know I have not fulfilled all that I am placed here to fulfill. I know I have not faced all the challenges that will come before me. I am running directly toward those challenges and those unknowns, as I am a human becoming, therefore, I am ready. I will always aspire for greater because greatness has no limits. He has no limits and I have no limits and His light has no bounds.

I submit to you that Greatness is calling. He is calling. Greatness beckons your commitment. He beckons your commitment. So, when God speaks to you, that "this life you have is your season," I want to encourage that you tremble not in fear of the unknown, but rather breathe heavily in the exuberance and excitement of His voice and His promise and walk in His light. Throughout this book, I am going to continually affirm in you what you really already know, but just may or may not be conscious of. Hence, I pray, Lord please let there be perspicacity in the metaphor, Greatness is a Shadow. It is my hope that this book reveals the greatness in you.

So, let's get started.

Chapter 2

It's EASY

"It's easy to do what it takes and it's easier not to do what it takes."

—*Barry M. Johnson*

When I think about the things that people say they want to accomplish in their lives, and in their business, or the journey people will embark upon to get from where they are to where they want to be, the *process* that's required to get there is easy. Yes, it is easy.

But, take a moment and just think about the way life and business constantly moves, constantly changes, perpetually operates and functions. Every day, people are bombarded with so many competing variables all at once. With so much going on around you, how is it that some people are able to rise above it and hit their mark while others struggle to just keep up. How can any of us walk in our purpose and fulfill our God-given greatness.

IT'S EASY

The result achieved is in direct correlation to the effort given in the process.

As I have worked with, mentored, coached and advised clients and young business professionals, I have come to realize that what it takes for them to get where they want to go is easy. The problem, however, is that although it *is* easy to do those things that are necessary to accomplish their goals, it's also easy *not* to do those things. And because it's easy either way, most people just fall off. Why? Because it's easier to do what you have always done. It's easier to remain in your comfort zone. So many of you that will read this type of book have already had successes in so many areas of your life. Accordingly, these successes have allowed you to create beliefs (both good and bad), opinions and views about yourself, and what you are or are not capable of and what you can and cannot do. Many times, these beliefs, opinions and views can be either limiting in nature or they can be liberating and boundless.

ALWAYS START WITH THE END-RESULT IN MIND

Over and over, what has worked for me is to **start with the end-result in mind**. So ask yourself, *Where is it that I want to go? What is it that I want to do? What is it that I'm trying to accomplish? Then,* once you answer these question(s), you must then "commit to the process" to achieve the end-result.

Once you have a vision for what the end-result is and what it looks like, you will mentally, visually, psychologically, and emotionally know, feel and attract that end result. Your mindset will now focus on what it takes to get there, and your actions will follow suit. Starting out with the *end-result* in your mind, you can plan accordingly. The plan involves a process of working backward.

WORK BACKWARD TO MOVE FORWARD.

Working backwards, allows you to strategize and come up with exactly what it will take to get to the desired end. Thinking about the END, you tell yourself, Ok, I want to accomplish X.

Working BACKWARDS, you think to yourself that in order for me to accomplish X, I will need to accomplish steps A, B, C, and D. Next, you drill down even further and ask yourself, "what do I have to do to accomplish A, B, C, and D", but you must be methodical and efficient in your analysis. More specifically, you ask,

What's it going to take to get A done?

It's going to take steps 1-5.

What's it going to take to get B done?

IT'S EASY

It's going to take steps 1-4.

What's it going to take to get C done?

It's going to take steps 1-7, and then steps 1-3 to accomplish D.

So, by starting with the end-result in mind, you will need to prepare your mind from the outset that it will take at minimum four things, i.e. A, B, C, and D, as well as its accompanying steps, to actually get to X – the end-result.

Let me give you an example. Let's say you make the decision to lose 10 pounds. You've got a big event coming up in two and a half months, so in the next 60 days you want to lose 10 pounds. That's the end-result or the end goal you wish to achieve.

Imagining yourself one-to-two dress or slacks size smaller, you ask yourself, while looking in the mirror, How am I going to lose 10 pounds?

Working BACKWARD, you think of at minimum four things that you need to do – right off the bat - that it will take to get those pounds off. You're excited, so you come up with your plan. You tell yourself:

I know I've got to eat right.

I know I've got to work out.

I know I've got to cut back on my sugar and my carb intake.

I know I've got to get a good night's rest every night.

That was easy, right? Yes, but then something happens as you think about taking the first step. Something called reality begins to set in as you contemplate the potential hindrances to accomplishing your goal. These hindrances are those beliefs, opinions and views that are limiting and restrictive. I want to first help you recognize and identify these beliefs in order that you might break through their restraints. Restraining beliefs will cause you to become dormant, frustrated and overwhelmed before you can even get started toward your goal.

For instance, you may think: How am I going to do this? I have to work all day, I've got to do homework with the kids, I've got church responsibilities, I have spousal responsibilities, I have classes... how am I going to do all these things?

Breaking it down further, you wonder: How am I going to cut sugar and carbs out my diet when I'm always running, always busy, always on the go? How am I going to do that? I grab what I can grab when I can grab it. I don't have time to cook every single day; I'm just grabbing quick meals and a lot of times it's fast food.

IT'S EASY

Almost hopeless now, you continue to ponder about what else you have to do: I have to work out. When am I going to find time to work out? How am I going to do that? For one thing, I don't have a gym membership, or maybe I have a gym membership, but I don't have time to go. Or maybe I have time to go, but I don't have anyone to watch the kids. Or maybe I can get someone to watch the kids, but what if the person who watches the kids can't help with the homework? Their homework has to get done, and I'm the one who usually helps the kids. How am I going to find time to go the gym when I have all these things in the way?

And then, lastly, quite frustrated, you say to yourself: I have to eat right, but I can't afford that. I'm already on a budget. I'm already living check to check. I'm already barely getting by. I can't afford to eat organic. I can't afford to buy whole foods. I can't afford to do the things that require me to eat right. I don't have money to buy protein shakes and those foods the magazines suggest for "eating right." The healthier the meal the more expensive it costs. How am I supposed to do that?

Ok, what just happened here? You started out hopeful with the end-result in mind: you wanted to lose 10 pounds. You named four things you needed to do, and if you could just do those four things, you would certainly lose the weight. But all these things have suddenly gotten in the way.

Please understand–

What trips you up is not the part about losing 10 pounds.

What trips you up is not the part about eating right.

What trips you up is not the fact that you need to cut sugar and carbs.

What trips you up is not the fact that you need to get more sleep.

No. You couldn't even get to those issues. Why? Because you had too many reasons, too many things getting in the way. Your beliefs, created from your experiences up until now, and the lens through which you typically look has you caught up in failure and fear of the unknown, before you can even begin. You have too many realistic and justifiable obstacles that are affecting why you couldn't accomplish your goal.

The sad thing about all the very real obstacles you have raised, is that you are correct about all of them. But the saddest thing, is not that you are right, but that because you are right and all the obstacles really do exist, that you will allow those things to block your blessing, limit your capacity to reach your goal and place limits on your possibilities.

IT'S EASY

Listen: it's easy to say that your goal is to lose 10 pounds. It's easy to decide you want to do it. But it's just as easy to come up with excuses for why you can't!

So, how do you overcome this seemingly inevitable state of being?

In order to get past this quandary, we must find a way to transform our relationship with ourselves. We must find a way to transform our relationship with what we believe. We must find a way to transform our relationship with the things we tell ourselves. Greatness is a Shadow is rooted in "gratefulness" and consciousness.

So, what is your starting point? Gratefulness and consciousness are the starting points that will equip you with everything you need to get past whatever obstacles hold you back. You can cast your greatness shadow on all of your limiting beliefs, limiting opinions and limiting views by closing your eyes, looking inward, to awaken your consciousness to discover new opportunities, new truths, new realities and overcome any obstacle or limiting view you might have told yourself.

Understand that if you are still carrying the baggage of your past mistakes and shortcomings, you have no room to receive the new blessings manifested by the glory of God. Your refusal to put old baggage away and claim that today is a new day, leaves no room for God to restore you. Your limiting beliefs in your mistakes of the past take up too much cargo space in your mind, body and spirit. Let's put the extraneous baggage down and dispose of it properly. We got what we needed from the lessons learned in those experiences and the rest is just miscellaneous. If you hold on to limiting beliefs, this restricts your willingness and ability to believe you deserve more. Do not allow feelings of unworthiness caused by mistakes of the past, to block your blessings of abundance. If you chase two rabbits, both will get away. You can chase the mistakes of your past, and claim them as your own. Or you can chase the promises of your future and walk in your purpose and transform you life.

JUST DECIDE

Here's what I know. In your comfort zone, it is easier to sleep an hour longer. In your greatness zone, it's easy to get up an hour earlier. Just decide, where do you want to be? I want another dimension. I want greatness. I want everything at the next level. Decide. In your decision, you will find focus. In your focus, you will take action. You must remember that we show our gratefulness and express or display gratitude or appreciation to God for his ray of light that illuminates inside us by how we "consciously" "decide" and choose to live our lives on a day to day basis.

IT'S EASY

THERE IS NOTHING MORE POWERFUL THAN A MADE UP MIND.

A made up mindset leads to the ability to make a Decision and then live it and own it. When I talk about a made up mindset, I am not speaking of what you just want. I am referring to a made up mindset of what you must have, what you will have and what is non-negotiable for you and your life. This type of mindset is another level of power over oneself and another level of gratefulness, that leads to another whole level of greatness.

Mindset is so much more than positive thinking and unicorns. A made up mindset converts problems to promises, crisis into peace, obstacles to opportunities, difficulties into understandings, and transforms excitement into action, words into actualization and barriers into breakthroughs. Mindset of this ilk is one comprised of gratefulness and spirited energy.

This type mindset is one that is internalized by the decision maker so much so that nothing else will do. This mindset allows you to live from a positon of strength and a posture of courage. This made up mindset causes you to be relentless in your pursuit, passionate in your desire and inspires you to dig deeper, go harder and reach further.

As you think about the Next Level in your life, ask what is important to you, what are you passionate about, what inspires you most, who most do you want to affect, and what impact do you want to have? The answers to these questions must be so much internalized by you that you have no choice but to be open, honest and transparent with yourself. The Decision that results from a made up mind requires you to Focus. Focus leads to consistent action. Consistent action shows up and is named commitment. Commitment is what creates the Result.

Once you've made up your mind and decided that you're going to do something, your actions and how you respond to adversity will be completely different. This level of greatness and consciousness can only come from a higher version of yourself. You are strong, you are capable, you are more than enough. Everything you are looking for is already in you, but it is only found in a deeper expression of your best self.

It is this deeper expression of yourself that allows you to now decide how you will reach your goals and respond to limiting beliefs as they occur. Now, when obstacles show up, so does a different version of you in how you respond. You will create your reality. You will not be denied. You will no longer let life happen to you, but you will happen to life. In the same scenario from before, a person who has **decided** that they will commit to the goal would say to themselves:

I'm going to have physical activity in my schedule. Since, I can't go to the gym, then before I go to bed tonight I am going to walk around the block for 20 minutes. Since I can't run a mile YET, then I am going to walk a mile. Instead of taking the elevator, I'll take the steps.

It's so much easier to push the elevator button. But, it's also easy to take the steps. The change in mindset changes a person's approach and their commitment to accomplish the goal. The end results will always inevitably live within each of our choices. Instead of concentrating on what couldn't be done, this person makes a decision to get it done. The mind is now made up. Mindset is key.

Then, every action forward is a purposeful action that is focused, incremental and specific. The decision allows you to capitalize on every one of those singular and isolated moments. Those moments where "choices" are made. Choices that make incremental and marginal progress in you and who you are becoming and that allow you to be the best and most authentic version of yourself. Every choice is aimed at getting it done, little by little, day by day and in spite of the perceived obstacles.

In the first scenario, the person may not have ever gotten started because the excuses, reasons and "valid" justifications that we allow to get in the way; the "I don't haves" become too overwhelming, too consuming . . . the cost and sacrifice is clearly too high or too much to bear. But nothing is too much for God. IF you are conscious of what is illuminating you on the inside, you see every obstacle as an opportunity to be creative and resourceful and get around it anyway.

Ultimately, we must decide what we're going to do, and what it is going to be. Then we make conscious choices, specific choices, intentional choices, purposeful choices, moment by moment of our day in order that we win the day! It is in our choices that live our results.

GREATNESS IS FOUND IN THE DAILY VICTORIES

I coach people to "Win the Day". Don't worry about losing 10 pounds. Let's concentrate on winning at breakfast; then, lets win at lunch. Next, we win at dinner. Win before you go to bed. Win the moment that you step out of bed. Win when you park the car. Just win today. These "wins" allow us to start a pattern of consistency and allows us to build momentum. Consistency and momentum will create a compound effect. Momentum occurs when you take the first step. It's sometimes hard, but you take it anyway. The first step sets you up to take the second step. The first step was hard, and the second was harder, but it gets easier. The results don't show up right away. You just have to keep showing up and putting in the work. Take the actions that lead you to the result in which you have committed. Commitment shows up dressed as consistency. Consistency looks in the mirror and sees the results of commitment. Its starts off hard, but it gets easier, and then it becomes automatic.

Focusing on winning the day, moment by moment, allows you to build momentum throughout the day and create achievements in all areas of your life including career, productivity, business, personal relationships, and more. In his monumental work "The Compound Effect," Darren Hardy suggests and demonstrates how small, purposeful, intentional, incremental choices of action, can exponentially multiply your likelihood of reaching your end result.

And remember this, your words absolutely matter. What you tell yourself matters. So be careful with your word choices when you set out to accomplish your goal. Your brain naturally responds in accord to the linguistics that you use. Don't say, "I need the exercise and the fresh air." Instead, say "**I am** going to get some exercise and enjoy the fresh air."

What's the difference? Just "needing" to do something does not make you do it. Recognition of the need does not create the mindset of getting it done. Students need to study, but many don't.

Smokers who are concerned about their health, know they need to stop smoking, yet they can't wait until the next smoke break. Procrastination sets in, desire sets in, distractions kick in, or maybe even perfectionism gets in your way. As my wife often says, "perfect is always the enemy of done." It is just as easy to not do what you need, as it is easy to do what you need. You will do it when the decision is made to get it done, not just because you need to do it.

Don't say, "I'm going to do what I can to win this morning with some type of physical activity before my day kicks in and my obligations take over." "Do what I can" and "some type of physical activity"; really? That is not specific. That is not purposeful. That is not intentional. Instead, say **I am** taking the dog for a walk or **I am** washing the car at 10am or **I am** cutting the grass today at noon; **I am** cleaning out the garage at 2pm. Stated in this manner, is specific, intentional, scheduled and purposeful and gets you your desired end result of physical activity and productivity.

Don't say "I can't have sugar or carbs." Instead say, I don't eat sugar or carbs. Why? Because "I can't have" is limiting and restrictive. It's psychologically the equivalent of punishing or depriving yourself. We always crave that which we "can't" have or are "not allowed" to have. But when you say, "I don't eat sugar," that is not restrictive, but rather it is your empowered decision. Still further, when you are intentional and unequivocal in your declaration, you are stating it now as if it already is, and therefore it shall be. Now that your words show up differently, you also show up differently. Your words are declared in strength, and you are seen as strong and resolute. Over time, what you now stand for and represent, you actually become. You inevitably transform into what you have declared to already exist. You have defined your reality in your words, which defines your reality in your actions and now its no longer a challenge to hang in there and be strong and disciplined because you have now owned who you are and how you show up.

You are in control and it is specific, intentional and purposeful. Your decision is full of the purpose in which you made it. It is specific to the goal you set to lose 10 pounds. It is intentional because it is not "I'm trying to limit carbs", instead its "I don't eat carbs." "Trying to limit carbs" leaves room for mistake or shortfall or makes it optional. The latter illustration "I don't eat carbs" empowers you to be stronger and more committed and unapologetic in your decision making.

See, so many people are worried about the end-result of losing 10 pounds because it's easy to set that as a goal, but it's also easy to come up with excuses for why they can't accomplish it. How hard or easy will it be to make the alarm clock go off an hour earlier? All you have to do is set it. Your demands for the day haven't started yet. Your texting, emailing and other responsibilities involving your family and/or work haven't started yet.

Why is this important? What's the difference here? The difference is that you chose differently; you made a decision for an end result to lose 10 pounds and based on that decision, you focused and took action to therefore get up earlier and at a specific time to do a specific and purposeful thing.

No matter the task or the challenge, just recognize that it's easy. It is just as easy *to do* what it takes, as it is **not** *to do* it what it takes. Once you know that your greatness is there inside you, then it's easy to acknowledge it, but it's also easy to ignore it. Think about how quickly you lose awareness of the presence of your shadow. Go ahead! Find it again, right now. Now choose to have the same deliberate attitude of awareness with your greatness.

Your greatness makes you shine. Your greatness emits your light. Your light allows you to cast your shadow of greatness upon everything you do and everyone you touch. So, you must be deliberate, purposeful and relentless to not allow obstacles, setbacks, lack of resources, doubters, and your own insecurities and limiting beliefs or disempowering words get in the way. Decide nothing and no one is going to dim your light. Dimness can make you fearful; dimness can make you want to run and hide. When I am feeling doubts of dimness on my light, I'm encouraged again and again by reading Marie Williamson's poem:

Our deepest fear is not that we are inadequate. Our deepest fear is that we are powerful beyond measure. It is our light, not our darkness that most frightens us. We ask ourselves, Who am I to be brilliant, gorgeous, talented, fabulous? Actually, who are you not to be? You are a child of God. Your playing small does not serve the world. There is nothing enlightened about shrinking so that other people won't feel insecure around you. We are all meant to shine, as children do. We were born to make manifest the glory of God that is within us. It's not just in some of us; it's in everyone. And as we let our own light shine, we unconsciously give other people permission to do the same. As we are liberated from our own fear, our presence automatically liberates others.

This poem speaks volumes in that we are often afraid of ourselves and the greatness that is within us. It's easy to hide behind fear; it's easy to give up on dreams. It is easy to quit, as soon as someone else attains a similar goal before we do. It is easy to let yourself think that God must not have wanted me to do that, or have that, and then we go and tell ourselves a story about why it did not happen for us. It's easy to stop eating right or exercising because the ten pounds didn't fall off in two weeks like you hoped it would. It's easy to give up on love, because someone broke your heart. It's easy to give up on dreams because those dreams did not become realized fast enough.

But it's also just as easy to step into the light and soak in the rays emanating from the light, or to close your eyes, look inwardly and consciously, and then walk in your greatness. It is easy to applaud those who accomplished their goals and you keep pressing on and striving with zeal toward the goals and God-ordained purpose intended for *you*.

So, Greatness is easy, but so is failure. With the same effort it takes to find your shadow, you will find your greatness. The moment you start putting forth effort, is the moment that consistency and commitment all of a sudden show up. Now you can begin to go to another dimension; another level, the next level. Now you can begin to actually see greatness as it is being manifested in you. Now, you can get a vision for greatness from a perspective never quite visualized until now.

Chapter **3**

Vision

*"In order to carry a positive action we must
develop here a positive vision."*

—*Dalai Lama*

As stated in Chapter 1, my purpose in this book, and
ultimately in this chapter, is to help you understand that
there is a process required in getting from where you are
to where you want to be. That *process* will determine
your *mindset*, your mindset will affect your *actions*, and
your actions will lead to your *greatness*.

Process ▸ Mindset ▸ Actions ▸ Greatness.

DECISIONS REQUIRE A VISION

The process cannot begin until you have created a
vision for yourself. In the last chapter, we discussed the
need to be able to "make a decision." Now that you have
made that decision, and your mindset is clear on what the

end result is going to look like, now you have to begin to take those steps in the direction of greatness and perform specific, purposeful, conscious day to day focused decisions that lead you to the actions of where you want to go.

So, the process really is that easy to do. The process is also really that easy, not to do. So what happens. Why is it easier not to do it? Why is it our comfort zone is stronger and more compelling than our greatness zone?

As we stated earlier, most people can't get there because the "process" becomes overwhelming. First, one must DECIDE. Then, the decision requires you to create a Vision and the Vision cannot be implemented without a Process. That Process is impossible to follow and endure if the "mindset" cannot make the daily choices, moment after moment, which are all the focused actions, which then leads to the commitment not being there, and in turn the day to day consistency is also not there; and nor will be the results.

Greatness is a Shadow will empower people to transform their lives and walk in their purpose. But, if it is easier not to walk in our purpose, then how can we prevent ourselves from choosing the same old path and the same old comfort zone? Get a clear vision.

The first mistake that people make when creating a vision for themselves, their life or specific areas of their life is that the vision is not clear. Instead, its vague. A vague vision is an amorphous vision. A vague vision is an elusive vision. A vague vision is merely a dream. It is nothing more than a pie in the sky. A vague vision is not a vision at all. One reason so many people struggle with finding clarity in their vision, is that it forces you out of your comfort zone and what you have grown accustomed to. So even though you may be miserable in your relationship or in your job and even though you may be miserable in other areas of your life. The fact remains that even in your misery, you have learned how to maneuver and exist in those miserable environments. The known misery is more comfortable than the unknown that comes with change. No, instead, your vision must be clear. Clear means clarity. Clarity requires an exactness. An exactness in your vision does more than give you just a picture of the goal, instead it provides a turn by turn navigation or direction toward that goal.

Remember, the next level of greatness in you is not a destination, but rather a process of becoming and transforming your life into who God intended for you to become. So then, clarity and exactness in your vision allows you to see and "live" in the very goal you have set. As you become it, you are it. As you move toward it, you are it. As it happens, during the process, it just begins to show up. The universe places you physically, mentally, spiritually, and psychologically into the realm of that end result as you are moving in the direction of those end results. As you do it, you become it.

Each moment is a new opportunity to submerse yourself into the environment of your future reality. This exactness is a virtual reality of sorts, where you put on the virtual reality glasses and suddenly you begin to see yourself in a place or in a space where reality as you once knew it no longer exists. Suddenly, now you have to maneuver in a way that adapts to your new virtual surroundings, because everything you see is not as you once saw it. Everything you are perceiving is causing pro-actions and reactions. Your frontal cortex is responding with feedback and innate triggers and reflexes and you are forced to move in a new way. The problem is that you still remember all the failures, all the limiting beliefs, all the opposition and all the things you previously did not get quite right. Don't run! Face it head on! Fear has no hold on you. Mistakes of the past were merely lessons from your past. You are a human becoming and irrespective of what limitations showed up in the past, you have chosen to operate at another frequency and another level.

Operating from this space puts you in a different place. Operating in this space will affect not only how you deal with yourself and your reality, but it will affect how you deal with everyone else. For example, one of my limiting beliefs and current realities is that I am historically (and possibly currently still) not a patient person. I have always had a low tolerance and thresholds of patience over the slightest things. I had to own up to that and recognize that about myself if I was ever going to become a better person. I have known its true from my past experiences. Therefore, when I communicate with people, I intentionally, specifically and purposefully enter into those communications with a made up mind about how I will empower myself to employ patience in my conversation, in my negotiation, in my trainings and in matters of life.

What is amazing is that I never knew that I could actually be "purposeful, specific and intentional" about changing my impatience and the resulting communications that resulted from that impatience. Then, when I met my wife, I experienced a type of love on a level unlike anything I knew was possible. Throughout our relationship, nothing mattered, or nothing bothered me, and nothing made me become impatient about anything. I am not saying we did not go through conflict or have engaging and different points of view about things important to us. That would not be realistic. What I am saying is that despite whatever was going on, that my love was so deep that I created a vision for what our love would look like unconditionally. My vision about this woman, and this relationship was so real, so deep and so vividly clear, that nothing mattered except being the best version of me possible in all things, especially in my perceived weaknesses of impatience and resulting communication. I DECIDED that I would only be a source of encouragement, inspiration, love, understanding and possibility with this woman. I DECIDED that EVERY communication with me would feed her spirit, her woman, her femininity, her heart, her passions, her feelings, her needs, her dreams and her wants. Through that DECISION, created by a vision of unconditional and unyielding love, I was able to "become" a better man and the one she would choose to be her husband and soul mate.

I remember a friend and his wife told me once that words are like nails. Once you drive them into someone, even if you pull them out, it still leaves the hole. Years later, nails removed and forgotten are still evidenced by the holes they left in the person's spirit, the person's confidence, and in the manifestation of what God had created them to be.

Accordingly, when I speak to my wife, I speak to her in the most empowering, respectful and genuine way. When I discipline our children, I speak to them in the most empowering, respectful and genuine way. When I think or talk to myself, I do it in the most empowering, respectful and genuine way. It is important that whatever the message gets communicated, but it is equally important that people I love, care about and come across are left whole and empowered after that communication. It was not easy, but I decided that before I speak on anything, I ask myself, which person is going to show up. Will I show up as the version of me that lives confined by his limiting beliefs that lurk in my darkness? Will I show up as the version of me that has decided to step out of my darkness, in between God's ray of light and cast a shadow of kindness, patience, understanding, love and appreciation.

When you step into the light, you too will cast your shadow. What will it look like? Get a vision for it. Decide. You and I always have a choice. There is no provocation that takes away our power to choose. Will I choose to be patient? Will I choose to be kind? Will I choose to be empowering? Will I choose to be encouraging? Will I choose to be understanding? Will I choose to be limited and confined and restricted to my past experiences and idiosyncrasies or will I choose to be open to receive what God has promised to me on this new day?

Greatness abounds in you. Get a vision for yourself, and whatever the next level in your life looks like, and decide that it is yours, then claim it and then act upon it. Now you begin to harness your past experiences and use them to your benefit instead of to your detriment.

VISION

For example, Financial freedom or wealth is an oft mention end-result or goal for people. Financial freedom is a motivation for a lot of people, including myself. So, once I DECIDED that financial freedom was a necessary and non-negotiable part of my life, only then, did my life begin to change.

However, in my earlier years, financial freedom was not a vision for my life. It was merely a paper chasing goal in my life. My definition of financial freedom was not defined, instead, it was more of a hope and an unrelenting want and that want, lacked any type of clarity as to what financial freedom really meant to me and what I wanted in my life. So my quest of financial freedom was nothing more than vague and ambiguous. It was associated with a particular dollar amount, or possessions of material objects. Interestingly, the more money I made the less financial freedom I actually had. Why? Because my vision of financial freedom was attached to an amorphous, abstract, pie in the sky dream of a dollar amount, but the dollar amount once reached; the cars once owned; the yacht once acquired; the watch once it was on my arm; the relationships I found myself in; the people around me that made up my circle; the type of fleeting and conditional love I shared with others; the people I wanted to affect; none of this gave me the universe of financial freedom that I ever really wanted. Ironically, everyone around me, applauded. The naysayers had become believers and the detractors were envious.

In their eyes, the abundance of perceived wealth created an allusion of financial freedom. The allusion it created for them was a mirror image of my vague and ambiguous pie in the sky dream. What they and I had each heretofore perceived as financial freedom were exact replicas of one another. Unfortunately, none of it was real. It was not a vision at all.

Oh, But God! But greatness, but my shadow, but my being, but His promise, but I was becoming. Today my vision of financial freedom is much more clear and specific. Financial freedom is about a very specific quality of life that is best exemplified through the vision I have for my lifestyle. Now, having a vision means the opportunity to enjoy the beauties of life. The power of a vision means replacing a lifestyle of survival, of lack, of loneliness, of getting by, of getting over, of settling for what is given instead of having expectancy for what you deserve.

Financial freedom means I live a healthy lifestyle. Financial freedom means I am actively engaged on a daily basis at having the freedom and the time to maintain being physically fit and taking care of my health.

VISION

Financial freedom means having options. One option is to wake up when I am done sleeping instead of to the sound of an alarm clock. Another option, is that when my feet hit the floor in the morning, I am not getting in rush hour traffic to serve some other master. Instead, I jump out of bed ready to serve The Master, my Father. I jump out of bed ready to serve myself, my body, my spirit, my mind, my nutrition, my health, my community, my family and my wife. When my feet hit the floor, my day is already ordered and its never the same. Forty-five minutes on a treadmill, followed by 45 minutes in the weight room, then fifteen minutes in the sauna, fifteen minutes in the jacuzzi, take a fifteen-minute shower and eat some breakfast. Spend time talking and experiencing the presence of God. I pray, do meditation, read and then write my affirmations and blessings. See, if I can achieve financial freedom, then I am in control of my time. The day is mine and every day is however different I choose for it to be.

This is part of what *wealth* looks like to me! I had to visualize it; I had to be able to get a vision of what it looked like. My vision of wealth includes the wholeness of being *fit* in mind, body and soul. So, the work I do – my grind, my hustle, my spiritual life – all align with God's purpose for me. Because of the *conscious effort* I put in EVERY DAY, my current universe now conforms to my vision, and I have been fortunate enough to see God's hand moving on my behalf.

As a result, wealth and financial freedom means that I **can** decide from any and all available choices about what's next in my life and where and how I will choose to spend my time. ***Wealth is about choices for me.***

Again, this is what financial freedom is to me; it's so much more than fancy cars, houses and stuff. Instead, wealth is empowering me to empower others. Wealth is my license to serve and give back. I had to visualize this result and see myself operating in it. Every time I step into a yoga studio to teach a class to a health conscious, spiritually grounded and vision driven, purposed-filled group of yogis, I am reminded of how wealthy, healthy and blessed I am. They turn to me to lead them, empower them and inspire a purpose centered intention for their mind, their body, their spirit, their movement, their balance, their stability, their stamina, their mindfulness, their breath and their being. The honor to serve in that capacity is what wealth and financial freedom looks like to me.

GET A MENTAL PICTURE OF YOUR GOAL

When I say you must get a vision for yourself, I want you to get a picture of what that looks like. Don't tell me you want to be rich; tell me what rich looks like! Don't tell me you want a successful business; tell me what success looks like! Many years ago, I heard Rev. John Jenkins preach a sermon from Proverbs 29:18 which states "Where there is no vision, the people perish". Rev. Jenkins brilliantly went on to take each letter in the word vision and make each of those letters applicable to the steps necessary to create a vision. The passages below represent my own personal spin on what Rev. Jenkins was teaching to the congregation.

GET A V-I-S-I-O-N FOR YOURSELF.

V - VISUALIZE

The first letter in the word vision is V which stands for **Visualize**. To visualize is *to create a mental picture* of what it is that you want. It can be a goal, dream, aspiration, a passion or something else, but picture it in your mind. What does it look like and how does your vision show up in other areas of your life?

Whatever your something is, try to get a vision for it. So many of us lack the ability to create a vision because of our lack of exposure. How does one begin to visualize something they can't even comprehend is possible? How can I get a vision for something that I have never seen or experienced? If you are not sure what it means to get a vision, then grab a magazine and imagine yourself in that place. Turn on the travel channel. Put yourself in a place where you can "see it."

YOUR V-CHALLENGE

Take some time and **write out** what your vision is. As your visualize your goal, dream, or aspiration, try to use **sensory words** to provide details of what that looks, feels, tastes, smells, and sounds like. Where in your life are your lacking a vision for yourself? **Is it in your Faith? Finance? Fitness? Family?**

Are you spiritually connected to a higher power? What is your vision for your spiritual life? Are you financially where you want to be and, in a position, to provide financial security to your family if something happened to you? What is your vision for your finances and what do you currently have in place to ensure you are reaching it? Are you physically where you want to be? Is your blood pressure within a safe zone? Are you at risk for heart disease or diabetes and who will be the person blessed to take care of you should you become ill? What is your vision for your health, fitness and wellbeing, now and in the future? What is your vision for your family relationships? With your spouse, significant other, your children, your siblings, your parents or those who you claim you love?

VISION

Please understand that until you have a vision for each area of your life, you can not possibly make the decision to reach a desired result.

I - INTERNALIZE

The second letter in the word *vision* is I which stands for **Internalize**. You have to internalize the vision.

You have to internalize it so much so, that you become one with that which you internalize. So much so that, "Woe unto you" if you choose not to internalize your vision.

In 1 Corinthians 9:16 Paul declares, *"Woe is **unto** me, if I preach not the gospel!"* It amazes me how Dr. R. L. Hymers, Jr. of Baptist Tabernacle of Los Angeles characterizes Paul:

Other than Christ Himself, the most important figure of the first century was the Apostle Paul. Paul was great in everything he did. Paul was a rebellious sinner, before he was converted, persecuting the early Christians. His conversion was also very great, with Christ Himself appearing to him. He then became a very great Christian, one of the greatest who ever lived. And he was the greatest preacher of all time. He preached in many nations in two languages, to both Jews and Gentiles. He preached before kings – to King Agrippa and to the Emperor Nero. Whatever Paul did, he did with all his heart, with intense zeal. Whenever he preached, he did it with all his might.

According to historical and biblical accounts, Paul did everything with a conscious, specific purposeful manner. Paul recognized and acknowledged the internal light that illuminated within him, and the gift of anointing to preach the Word, he had been bestowed. And so, Paul emphatically declared "Woe is unto me if I don't preach the gospel!" That is precisely the way I mean for you to think about *what* and *how* you are to internalize what you visualize.

You have to internalize what you have visualized so much so that you become one with it. But understand that the oneness you begin to realize will get stronger as you do what you are called to do."

So whether it is becoming wealthy, creating a successful business, being a good parent, reaching peak physical fitness, whatever the vision is that you set, is inherently what God wants for you anyway. Each of us has a unique task and talent that God desires to use in us so that His greater works may be fulfilled on earth. What He has for *you*, is for *you*.

You can't visualize something that you weren't created by God to do.

Keep in mind that **God desires that you be free from debt and free from health issues**:

VISION

> "*Dear friend, I pray that you may enjoy good health and that all may go well with you, even as your soul is getting along well*" (3 John 1:2 NIV).

He desires that you be stress free and seek harmony and balance with each other and with the earth:

> "*And God is able to bless you abundantly, so that in all things at all times, having all that you need, you will abound in every good work*" (2 Corinthians 9:8 NIV).

He also desires that you be a lender and give of yourself cheerfully and freely instead of being a beggar and a borrower:

> "*Give, and it will be given to you. A good measure, pressed down, shaken together and running over, will be poured into your lap. For with the measure you use, it will be measured to you*" (Luke 6:38 NIV).

Each of us, then, has the same promise offered to us from God, but each of us needs to know that we are worthy of such blessings. In order to operate in our gifting and purpose, we have to put forth the effort to do it. In order to put forth the effort, we must internalize what we have visualized. We cannot achieve our greatness unless we start by visualizing ourselves having reached that end result first. Then, as we discussed earlier, we must work backward to plan small achievable goals and to win daily at those things. *If you can see it, you can achieve it.*

If you are visualizing and internalizing what does NOT line up with what God has for you, no matter how big your vision is, again, you'll never get it. God's will for *you* is blessed and is in *you*. Breathed into *you*. Placed in *you*. He's the One that gives you the vision and that's why and how you're able to visualize it. If you have a oneness with it – *it* being your purpose or what God has breathed into you -- you won't be able to stop the manifestation being lived out in you.

But I can't create the vision for you. No, that can't happen, nor should it be an expectation for this book. Let's say, though, that you ran after what *you* wanted, even if you thought it was good and would be a blessing to people, but that was not what God wanted for you and you failed at what you tried to accomplish.

That's okay. Why? Because even though your journey may not have turned out the way you wanted, or maybe you ran into all kinds of complications in the steps you took on your way to get there, the reality is that you learned valuable lessons and stumbled into what God had been preparing for you all along. It is *now* at this new point of awareness that you can possibly begin to walk in your vision, the vision that God put there, that you can clearly see now. It is *now* at this new place that you can walk in what you've internalized and visualized which equates to walking in your purpose. You won't get to your purpose until you decide it is yours. You will recognize an internalized spirit when it settles deep inside the core of your innermost being. The internalized spirit will be rooted in your mind, your body and your spirit so much so that your emotions and mindset are only content when operating inside this space.

YOUR I-CHALLENGE

Take time to **write out** the internalized discoveries of your vision. Discuss your "Woe is unto me" gift or talent that **must be** shared with the world.

Where in your life is your vision so strong that you have either internalized or you know that you need to begin to internalize and become one with that vision.

Are you spiritually connected and in oneness to a higher power? What have you internalized for your spiritual life? Are you financially where you want to be and in a position to provide financial security to your family if something happened to you? What have you chosen to internalize to see to it that your vision for your finances comes to fruition. What do you currently have in place that evidences how you have internalized your vision rather than just speaking to it and that ensures you will reach it? Are you physically where you want to be?

Is your blood pressure within a safe zone? Are you at risk for heart disease or diabetes and who will be the person blessed to take care of you should you become ill? What is your internalized commitment toward your vision for your health, fitness and wellbeing, now and in the future? How is that internalized spirit evidenced through what you do consistently rather than what you talk about doing? What have you internalized your vision for your familial relationships? With your spouse, significant other, your children, your siblings, your parents or those who you claim you love? How is it evidenced? If asked, how would each of the people you love describe the things that evidence how you have internalized what you profess your vision to be?

Please understand that until you have internalized a vision for each area of your life, you cannot possibly make the decision to reach any desired result in that area of your life.

S - STRATEGIZE

The third letter in the word *vision* is S which" stands for **Strategize**. You must have a strategy or make a plan to achieve the internalized vision. There are so many books that have been written on the subject of strategy, because planning is one of the most critical stages of any process, in any career, in any course or path of life.

VISION

When this project first began I was working with a long-time childhood friend that I chose to be my editor on this project. So, when this book began to unfold and materialize, we had to strategize in order to try to bring this book to fruition. During that time she was a full-time associate professor of English and Humanities at one university, also serving as an adjunct at the local community college, while raising three children, and supporting a recording gospel artist husband in his career.

*But not doing this, not accomplishing this project was **not** an option.*

So, she pushed because she wanted to fulfill a lifelong dream, but also because her then current professor position was going to no longer be available due to budget cuts. So even with all the demands of her life, she now felt pressure in a new and different way. In just a few months after we started, she would be faced with no job.

I use her story as an example for you because she wanted her life and experiences to be revealed in full and transparent manner so that others may benefit from what she learned. Ironically, while she worked on this project for me, she herself became a project of the project. In other words, she found herself utilizing every aspects of this book to move her from where she was at that time to where she wanted to be. Only God could have orchestrated that!

Before we started one of the recording sessions for this book, I told her that she needed to strategize more about her plans to start and run her publishing company full-time. She always had this tremendous dream of being the voice for people who have a story to tell, which means she would be writing their books and possibly publishing them as well. That is an awesome *why* and *purpose* that she had been holding onto for almost 20 years. When she told me that, I began to treat her as if I were her business mentor or coach. She could already visualize what she wanted to do, but now she needed to internalize it and then strategize for it. I wanted her to know what stepping out in the ray of light of business ownership was like; I wanted her to see it. I wanted her to internalize the vision of feeling the pages of each book she was going to write and publish, including possibly editing my book. I told her to hold it in her hands and to visualize each book as already being a *New York Times* best seller.

So, for this particular project, we had to strategize around every potential hindrance, every potential obstacle, and on how we were going to do it in spite of or despite those things.

VISION

In the end, God a had a different plan and gave me a different vision. I abandoned for nearly 2 years writing this book. The inspiration I first had on the original manuscript was lost, and so I started over and found my voice and I strategized, this time alone, about how I would get it done. Now, praise God, here we are.

YOUR S-CHALLENGE

Take time at the end of this chapter to **write out** what you feel are the strategic steps necessary to get you where you need to be. Anticipate hindrances and obstacles. Name them one by one, and then develop a strategy around each.

I - IMPLEMENT

The fourth letter in the word *vision* is I – **Implement**. After you have a strategy, you've got to implement that strategy. Having a strategy is not enough; you must have an executable strategy. If it's not executable, you will end up spinning your wheels. You'll end up being very busy but accomplishing nothing.

> *"Many people fail in life, not for lack of ability or brains or even courage, but simply because they have never organized their energies around a goal." Elbert Hubbard, American philosopher and writer*

Again, the purpose of a strategy is to get you to this stage – implementation – because it's your strategy that will make it executable.

Let's say you don't have enough money to implement your dream, goal or aspiration. So what? You're going to have to be more creative. Let's say we're business partners and we don't have enough money to complete a project. So what? We're going to have to identify and rely on some other resources. We're going to have to use what we've got. We say we can't meet at five thirty like we planned. Ok, so what? We can reschedule and do it at eight. If that's inconvenient, we do it at nine. So what? We are going to overcome any obstacle that comes up. Why? Because *stuff* is going to happen. We can't get stuck on what we don't have or what we would've, could've, should've done. We must literally find a way to get around whatever comes up and attempts to block our goals.

In addition, we must set a measurable plan of execution and begin to establish SMART goals (specific, measurable, achievable, relevant, time-bound), and do SWOT analysis (strengths and weaknesses, opportunities and threats), to keep us moving forward.

There are several effective methods to help implement goals and to measure progress. Several websites offer online charts that have been designed for people to plan and implement. With so many tools available, there is no need for us to be casual about what it is we want to do. It requires effort – there it is again – on our part to make it happen.

Personally, for every venture I propose in my life, I consistently use the SWOT analysis to explore every possible angle.

YOUR I-CHALLENGE

Take time at the end of this chapter to **write out** the actionable executable steps toward accomplishing your goal. Use either or both of the S.M.A.R.T. goals and S.W.O.T. analysis templates to help you think through and overcome limitations and obstacles.

O - OVERCOME OBSTACLES

The fifth letter in the word vision is **O**. We've got to **Overcome Obstacles**. The fact that obstacles always happen, lets me know that I can count on obstacles *to* happen. But I also know that every time I look for my shadow, I actually find it. The consciousness of my internal light and my "all-in" mindset, lets me know that when things happen, I am prepared. All my failures up until now, along with all my successes have prepared me for whatever obstacle may present itself.

I knew that obstacles would happen when I created the vision, but I also knew that no weapon formed against me would prosper. That faith is what allows me to even create the vision in the first place. I knew that when I internalized His will and I knew that when I set my strategy that their would be obstacles and I knew that I would overcome them in spite of their existence. We already know that's going to happen. But what story are you gonna tell yourself. Experience tells us. Life teaches us that things are gonna happen. You're going to have to overcome obstacles and get it done by necessity. It's just part of the Process.

YOUR O-CHALLENGE

Take time at the end of this chapter to **identify** the obstacles or hurdles, historically, that have always gotten in your way. Be honest in naming them, and then indicate *why* they have been obstacles and what you must do to overcome them by any means necessary. I will warn you that it is hard to be honest with yourself. Lean on the light the radiates upon you and inside you. Light reveals.

N – NECESSITATE CHANGE NOW!

The sixth and final letter in the word *vision* is **N**, which stands for the **necessary changes** we must make. Why? Because not overcoming the obstacles, not getting where you need to be, not implementing the strategy, not strategizing something that's executable, not internalizing what God is telling us, not stepping into our vision, not casting our bodies in between His rays of light . . . **not** doing those things, is **<u>not</u>** an option. It must be done by necessity. No matter what and now.

Your mindset will require a change.

There's no way that you can expect a different outcome if you keep doing things the same way you've always done them. There's no way. It's insane to think that sleeping late every day, procrastinating, eating the same carbs, sleeping only one to two hours per night, not exercising, and so on, is going to get you the results you desire.

Process ⸳ Mindset ⸳ Actions ⸳ Greatness

Joyce Meyer wrote a powerful book entitled *Battlefield of the Mind*, and in it, she discusses how people's minds are battlefields. We are constantly waging wars within ourselves about how we perceive things, and those perceptions keep us from moving forward. She says that this war is precipitated by the devil. Meyer emphatically states,

The devil is a liar. Jesus called him *"the father of lies and of all that is false"* (John 8:44). He lies to you and me. He tells us things about ourselves, about other people and about circumstances that are just not true. He does not, however, tell us the entire lie all at one time.

He begins by bombarding our mind with a cleverly devised pattern of little nagging thoughts, suspicions, doubts, fears, wonderings, reasoning and theories. He moves slowly and cautiously. Remember, he has a strategy for his warfare. He has studied us for a long time.

He knows what we like and what we don't like. He knows our insecurities, our weaknesses and our fears. He knows what bothers us most. He is willing to invest any amount of time it takes to defeat us. One of the devil's strong points is patience.

Thus, the longer our mind is at war, the farther we are away from walking in our God-given purpose. You've got to change your mind!

So again, understanding that our daily processes are driven by our mindset, if we set a goal that will alter or change our normal process, it will require a shift or change in our mindset as well, because we will not be able to accomplish our goal doing things the same way we have always done them. You can't maintain the status quo and expect a different outcome.

*It is ONLY when our mindset changes that we will be able to **commit** to a different process.*

YOUR N-CHALLENGE

Take time at the end of this chapter to **write or draw** out any processes that you know MUST change. What will those changes require? Be honest with yourself.

So, take action! This is **your** vision that we're talking about. V*ision* is a **verb**—an action word! I want you to get a vision. See it for yourself, and then take action.

- Visualize
- Internalize
- Strategize
- Implement
- Overcome obstacles
- Necessitate change *NOW*.

GOD KNEW WHAT ADAM WOULD CHOOSE

In Genesis 2, we are told that there were two trees in the Garden of Eden--the Tree of the Knowledge of Good and Evil and the Tree of Life. The text proves we have free will grounded in our available options. If there were not two trees, there would have been no choice to be made.

Adam made a choice. Whether we like it or not, his choice to eat from the Tree of the Knowledge of Good and Evil created an independence in us. With Adam's choice, there were consequences, but those consequences opened up new opportunities, new responsibilities, new parameters for how to live a life separate from God. God knew this would happen. So, He offers His light to us, to shelter us, to imbue us with the capacity to endure all of life's idiosyncrasies, and to pour *greatness* into us.

In all of this, I need for you to understand that all of us are equipped with the ability to make a decision, but through nature or through nurture or through biblical or historical precedence . . . however you want to say it, we ultimately have to decide.

SO, CHOOSE WELL MY FRIEND

You have to make a decision about *something* every day of your life. As you think about choices you have to make concerning your goals, dreams, and aspirations and getting from where you are to where you want to be, please know that you have greatness in you! A lot of things that you choose to do will be successful because there is greatness in you. It shows up on its own because you have an internal ray of light that casts your shadow even when you are unaware.

Get a vision for yourself and be sure the vision you get is consistent with God's will and not deviation from

VISION

His will. When you have a vision and it's not used for the purpose He breathed into you, you end up seeing glimpses of this greatness, stepping and walking in these glimpses of this greatness, but never, ever reaching your full potential. Never ever finding your breakthrough. Never ever getting to that ever-elusive goal that you set for yourself, and not reaching the goal that He set for you.

Yet even when or if your vision gets blurred and you fall away from God's will and choose to do your own thing outside of Him, just know that your greatness is still there, and so is your shadow.

V – VISUALIZE

CHALLENGE YOURSELF

Use this page to **draw** or **map out** what you visualize as your goal, dream, or aspiration. Then use **sensory words** to provide details of what that looks, feels, tastes, smells, and sounds like.

I – INTERNALIZE

CHALLENGE YOURSELF

Use this page to **write or draw out** the internalized discoveries of your vision. Discuss your "Woe is unto me" gift or talent that **must be** shared with the world.

S – STRATEGIZE

CHALLENGE YOURSELF

Use this page to **write out** what you feel are the steps necessary to get you where you need to be. Anticipate hindrances and obstacles. Name them one by one, and then develop a strategy around each.

I – IMPLEMENT

CHALLENGE YOURSELF

Use this page to **write out** the actionable executable steps toward accomplishing your goal. Use either or both of the S.M.A.R.T. goals and S.W.O.T. analysis templates to help you think through and past limitations and obstacles.

O – OVERCOME OBSTACLES

CHALLENGE YOURSELF

Use this page to identify the obstacles or hurdles, historically, that have always gotten in your way. Be honest in naming them, and then indicate why they have been obstacles and what you must do to overcome them by any means necessary.

N – Necessitate Change

CHALLENGE YOURSELF

Use this page to **write or draw** out any processes that you know MUST change. What will changing those processes entail? Be honest with yourself.

Chapter **4**

Failure Endurance

"The sky is not my limit...I am."

— T.F. Hodge, *From Within I Rise: Spiritual Triumph Over Death and Conscious Encounters with "The Divine Presence"*

There are a couple of ways we can think about failure endurance. If we start with endurance, what we typically mean is how resilient a person is. What is their staying power? How long can they last? We could be talking about running a race, swimming under water, getting on a treadmill, or just going through life.

The context I'm referring to, however, is specifically about your **failure** endurance. That is the endurance of how many times you can continue to fail and keep moving forward? Failures can steal life if we let them.

Something may not go quite the way we expected it to. Something may not have happened as quickly as we would have liked for it to. We may have wanted to lose weight, but the weight didn't fall off as quickly. We worked out for six months. We were diligent. We were doing our thing, yet we still did not see the results we wanted.

Unfortunately, at some point for many people, they will stop working on themselves. They'll stop growing. They'll stop dreaming. They'll stop pressing, pushing forward. They'll stop fighting.

I believe that death begins when growth stops and opportunity and possibility no longer exist in our lives. When growth stops, possibility stops. If you're not growing, then there is no possibility of getting anywhere closer to where you want to be. In order to get where you want to go, you have to be willing to become different from who you currently are and move beyond where you currently are. *Who you are* has gotten you to this point. But if you seek to live life on another level, then you have to be willing to change.

THE LIMITATIONS UPON CHANGE.

It is important to now this about change, we can change our circumstances by getting divorced, quitting our jobs, getting an education or learning something new. The reality, however, is that YOU are the common denominator between your current reality and your future reality created by these changes.

A new relationship will end with the same result, unless you change. A new job will end up with the same result, unless you change. A new skillset will result in the same results as your last learned skillset unless you change. You are the common denominator in your reality. The change you seek on the outside and around you, must first take place on the inside and within your mindset. Inevitably, our actions, limiting beliefs, ways of communication, and past are carried with us into our new situation. So real change, that will manifest itself on the outside of our life and the environment in which we live, must first be facilitated and manifested on the inside, and the spirit and mindset from which we come. We must decide to be a human becoming instead of a human being. Human beings live where they are. Human beings refuse to leave their comfort zone. Leaving their comfort zone is fraught with fear. A human becoming, relates to all aspects of life differently, so they live in growth and expansion and possibility, irrespective of their environment. Their reality becomes what they create, rather than what we see. The world of a human becoming becomes changed because how they feel, think, view, perceive, listen and respond has changed. Although their environment or circumstances may not have changed, but how they deal with it has. Instead of shifting things around you, you shift how you respond to the things that are around you.

THE FULFILLING POWER OF BEING OPEN AND AUTHENTIC

None of us are capable of resonating or vibrating on a higher frequency, or another level, until and unless we allow ourselves to be open to receive the greatness that is in us. Earlier on we talked about gratefulness, and how gratefulness, was a condition precedent to greatness. Gratefulness allows no room for narcissism or conceit or arrogance. Confidence is divine, while arrogance is ignorance. Many of us limit our access to the greatness within us, because we are shrouded in arrogance of who we think we are already. Learning to step out of our arrogance, or sometimes finding the humility to step out of arrogance, opens us up to receive the power and manifestations of our truest potential greatness. But so many people refuse to ever admit their inadequacies, shortcomings, faults and imperfections. Growth is not possible where authenticity and genuine honesty with ourselves does not seem to exist. Because we have reached some level of notoriety in our community, our school, our church, our book club, our job or on social media, we fail to even be open to the idea that we are not where we could be, especially if we are farther along than the people we surround ourselves with.

How many of us hide behind our fancy cars, our big houses and our name brands to appear bigger to ourselves and those around us? How many of us hide behind our education, corporate titles and big careers to appear bigger to ourselves and those around us? How many of us define ourselves by what we own and what we do for a living? What is it about designer brands, education, big vocabularies, material possessions, tight jeans or the shortest shorts and naked Instagram posts that empowers us to feel so good about ourselves? Why is social media a platform for our greatest accomplishments, rather than our honest fears? Why is it that we insist that everyone know how well we are doing, how good we look, and how much we spent. Why is it that we show off our comfort zones, and hide our struggle zones? Some of us are not showing off at all, but are just happy to be where we are because it may be further than we ever thought possible. Even then, some of us will resolve that even though things may not be great, they are better than they were and better than those around me, so I just want to maintain. Maintenance is not progression. Maintenance is stagnancy. Maintenance is not ascension, maintenance is complacency. Why would any one of us settle for just getting by. Why settle for just enough? Why settle for just to be better than where we once were, thereby denying the power of God's presence in our lives to take us to another level?

FAILURE ENDURANCE

Notwithstanding the aforementioned, consider that some of us feel like because we may have it together in one area of life, such as our followers on social media, or our job, or the car we drive, that we just do not have time to place value on other areas of our life that we KNOW we need to improve. What would it mean to have a good job and not know your children? What would it mean to make a lot of money, but have a failing marriage? What does it serve, for your ends to be met, but you have no capacity to ever help anyone outside of your household, family or otherwise during their time of need. Not only is it shortsighted, its selfish. Proverbs 21:2 "every man's way is right in his own eyes…"

Lastly, how many of us are "waiting for the right time" to do anything and everything. You find urgency in nothing at all. You are waiting to lose weight, but are genetically predisposed to be urgently rushed to the hospital. You are waiting to get acquainted with your kids, but urgently rushing to get to them to save them from some trouble that could have been prevented. You are waiting to build and improve your failing marriage, but urgently rushing to get out of the house so you can find peace in your spirit anywhere but at home. There is no right time. Tomorrow is not promised. Tomorrow never comes. When you wake up in the morning, it will be today. Tomorrow does not exist. All we have is now. Each moment, each breath, each action, is an opportunity to be purposeful, specific and intentional about how we will live our lives. Proverbs 6:9 "How long will you lie there? When will you get up from your sleep?...poverty will come on you like a bandit and scarcity like an armed man." Every day that you let go by, forces you to replace the joy and majesty of life and living with the mere redundancy and monotony of just getting by and despair.

My prayer and my hope is that every reader of this book will choose to embrace life to the fullest and always be learning and always becoming. In times such as these none of us can afford to show up merely as zombies who can physically move around, are filled with nothing and that are spiritually dead.

Greatness is a Shadow is a platform in which you no longer have to hide. Greatness is a Shadow encourages you to 10X every area of your life that YOU decide that you want to improve. 10X means setting a goal and working toward it every day to do better, be better, and continually become the best, truest, most authentic version of yourself. 10X yourself means releasing power within yourself and giving yourself permission to embrace everyday as if it were your last, and to impact every circumstance as your best truest and most authentic self only can. When you 10X your life in the areas that matter most to you, you create a 10X society all around you. Everyone you interact with, do business with, spend time with, communicate with, build with, explore with, love with and anything else with are constantly feeling your energy and your vibration and the spirit that reverberates around you and abounds within you. In order to 10X your life, you have to ask honestly yourself, Who do I really want to be? What are the things that matter most to me in life? What kind of man or woman do I want to be? What do I want to represent in my home, in my family and in my community? What shadow do I want to cast upon those around me? What energy do I want people to feel in my presence? When you can honestly answer these questions, you will enable yourself to create the life you want and that life will be empowered with a new strength, confidence and resolve.

I want to be fully empowered in all areas of my life that are important to me. I am not trying to tell you what should be important to you, but whatever you decide it is, why not be fully empowered in that space. Authenticity, transparency and genuine means vulnerable to most. But no. Authenticity, transparency and genuine means keeping it real in spite of the seemingly vulnerability and thereby releasing and making room for your greatness and your shadow and that next level in you and in your life. See, if you are filled with fear about authenticity in who you really are, and transparency about your life, it forces you to hide in the darkness and wear a mask to conceal your potential greatness. Hiding removes the risk and lessens the fear.

But when you step out of hiding in the darkness and step into God's internal light within you, you allow your shadow to be cast on the circumstances and people all around you and the things that matter most. Because you moved in spite of the risk, you embraced your fear, and the risk are now gone, and a greater expression of you becomes available and a power of greatness you have never seen. In essence, you become transformed and the people around you are now given permission to resonate with you on another level, a deeper, more authentic level and gives them permission to know that they can do the same.

CHANGE REQUIRES GROWTH.

Growth is only inspired, motivated, and accelerated because of the possibility of where it is that we are trying to go. Where possibility ends, growth stops and death begins. That's why failure endurance is so important. You must have the ability to overcome fear and endure the failures that are going to come. And let me tell you, both fear and failure are going to come. Commitment to live at the Next Level, does not mean fear and failure are not going to come, it means we are not going to quit when it does.

FEAR AND FAILURE IS GOING TO COME

If you're an entrepreneur, fear, failure and problems are going to come. If you're a parent, then fear, failure and problems are going to come. If you're a spouse, then fear, failure and problems are going to come. If you are a student, then fear, failure and problems are going to come. If you plan on having any meaningful relationships with someone, then fear, failure and problems are going to come. If you have any aspiration to accomplish anything at all in your life, then fear, failure and problems are going to come. Fear, failure and problems MUST come because fear and failure are necessary ingredients toward success.

As you pursue your vision, seek your goals and go after your destiny, you are going to get tested. You are going to get challenged. You are going to get pushed down. You're going to get lied too. Someone is going to stray from you. Someone is going to be disloyal to you. Someone is going to be unfaithful to you. Someone is going to cheat on you. Someone is going to do something behind your back. Someone is going to let you down.

All of these failures eventually begin to wear you out and wear you down. What happens when people get worn out or worn down? They stop working, they stop growing. Why? Because their endurance is weakening and they fear making the same mistakes again.

Vulnerability, is the fear that blocks love. So within your relationship, when your endurance weakens, is when most people are more likely to quit. But as your endurance weakens, your faith and belief must be continuously strong. Transforming your life to walk in your purpose requires that when it is dark and we can no longer see, and our circumstances have become so bad, is when we must remember Psalm 30:5, weeping may endure for a night, but that joy cometh in the morning.

Sometimes as life unfolds, we feel like we are in a nightmare. Many times we feel as though there is nothing we can do about a situation. Has it ever been so bad that seconds seem like minutes, minutes seem like hours and hours seem like days? Remember this, that even in our darkest hour, the pain only last but sixty minutes. Joy does cometh in the morning. Dr. King once said the ultimate measure of a man is not what he does during times of comfort and convenience, but what he does during times of trouble and controversy. Faith can not be tested, nor made strong only during the good times, but it must be tested, during the dark, cloudy and ominous times.

It is in times like these, where we must remember Romans 8:28, that "ALL THINGS... work together...for good." We were never promised in this verse that everything good would happen, no! It says "all things...work together...for good".

FAILURE ENDURANCE

Have you ever tried to go for a run? Then, at some point during the run, you tell yourself, "I can't go anymore. I need to just stop for a minute to catch my breath." Then, once you stop, at that very moment, you then begin to evaluate what is really happening. You ask yourself, *Am I resting or am I stopping? Am I just gathering my second wind or am I stopping?* Failure endurance makes you ask yourself these same questions and your commitment to your vision, causes you to get back up and get into the race. Failure endurance asks, *how long can you go before you quit*? Why? Because when you quit, you fail. When people's endurance becomes weaker, failure sets in because that's when they want to quit, so they stop working, stop growing, stop pushing, and stop fighting to get to the top.

FEAR IS ALSO A LACK OF ENDURANCE

Another word I like to use in place of failure endurance is the word *fear*. I think that most people are afraid of failure, because they know they have no endurance. So, they are afraid.

See, it is easy to tell everybody else what you are going to do. You can say, "I'm going to do it." "I'm going to get up in the morning at 5am." "I'm going to run 5 miles today." " I'm going to spend 50 hours a week at work." See, no matter what it is that you say you are going to do, the truth is that *you know* what your endurance looks like. *You know* when you're becoming weaker and fearful of achieving your goal.

Fear is the biggest deterrent to success.

Your fear is predicated on your knowledge of your past self and your past endurance. The challenge we have is that we cannot allow the realities of our fear to call those realities into existence. As those realities begin to show up it will immediately diminish your energy and sabotage your momentum. It's one thing to tell you *not* to be afraid; it's another thing to tell you **how** *not* to be afraid. I want you to move from where you are to where you want to be. You can increase your failure endurance, and you must, because failures are going to happen. The question is, *how much of it will you be able to endure*?

I want to dismantle your fear. But what's going to make your fear become less? What's going to weaken your fear? What's going to strengthen your ability to face your fear? *You have to know that your endurance is getting stronger.*

STOP ENDURING. START EMBRACING.

How does one strengthen their endurance? You stop enduring, and you start embracing. Stop enduring failures. When you endure something you take it on, as if it is yours to endure. You go through it, and when you go through it, it wears you out and it depletes you. That's why you need endurance; you need longevity. You're going to get winded; you're going to get tired. *You can either go through it, or you can grow through it.*

If we stop enduring failure and instead start embracing failure. *But, what's the difference? How do I stop?* The difference is in your mind. The difference is in how you perceive what is going on. No matter the circumstances or the conditions, you will begin to approach these things just like you approached your shadow. You cannot change the conditions, you cannot change what people will do and say to you, you cannot change your past, you cannot change what will happen to you, but ONLY YOU can change your mind, your attitude and how you approach, handle and deal with these things as they happen. You stop going through it, and you start growing through it. God tells us that no matter how much evil is upon us, nor how much suffering we seem to experience, that He makes all things new Revelation 21:5, "Behold, I make all things new." Enduring what happens to us makes us live and requires us to live in the presence of our own humanity and limitations with independence from God, but embracing what happens to us, makes us live and requires us to be mindful that it is a new day, and "behold", because "He makes all things new" that we are not to be conformed of this age, but to be transformed by the renewing of our minds. The transformation, in our minds allows us to see the light within all of us, and to step toward and into that light, so that we might cast a shadow of God's presence in us and in our lives, and the shadow we cast allows us to show up as a new person, with a renewing of our minds, and it affects how we show up to the circumstances, rather than how the circumstances will show up in us. Failure is going to happen, fear is going to happen, and when it does, **love it, embrace it, step into and in front of it,** and get real up close and personal with it. Have a NO MATTER WHAT approach to how you see it in your mind. Then, cast your shadow of greatness upon it and watch how your circumstances now begin to unfold, and the effects of the presence of you, which is the effect of the presence of God, because it is the higher iteration of you, the God in you, now makes all things new.

THE NO MATTER WHAT APPROACH TO SUCCESS

I'm inviting you to take a different approach and that approach begins in your mind. Don't be afraid of failure, instead embrace failure. You've always given up; you've always accepted fear and given in to it, over and over again. Maybe not in everything, because you are a fighter, a winner and you have come this far. But, "Behold, I make ALL things new" (emphasis added). So even though you have confronted some or many of your fears, I want you now to be transformed with a renewing of your mind, that you can face ALL fears. We no longer have to give in to fear. You may know from your past failures that your endurance is weak or that it can be sometimes. But do not internalize this as if you have to endure those past experiences as though they are who you are.

That type of internalization process can be problematic concerning fear because of what happens to us over the course of our lifetime. Here's what I know: People get beaten up by life. When we have been beaten up by life, guess what? It hurts. So yes, we already know what pain feels like. Why? Because you're probably in pain right now. We know what a broken heart feels like. Your heart may be broken right now.

Yet, in spite it all, you are still here. So, look at what you've overcome. Look at where you've come from. Look at the mistakes you've made. Look at your life in terms of how far you've come. Look at where you are and compare it to where you used to be. Look at where you are, and think about your vision of where you are now trying to go.

Behold, I make all things new. Don't give up. Hold on. Hold on to your dreams. Hold on to your faith. Hold on to growing and know that you are always becoming. Feel the earth's gravity and know that God is real, and that God is in you, and that you must cast your shadow.

You should pray to God like it depends on Him, but work like it depends on you. I want you to keep pushing, keep running, keep moving forward, keep working. I know you've been beaten up. I know it hurts, but the only way for you to move from where you are to where you want to be is you've got to embrace failure.

THE STRUGGLE IS REAL

Do you ever wonder why some people run and hide when failure hits, and why some people look failure in the face and step into it? Instead of running from what we fear. What can we do to prepare you to press forward? How much more do you need to do before you decide that you want to move forward anyway? How and what can we do to teach ourselves how to fight and how to endure? Fear exist in us all, but courage gives us the strength to press forward in spite of fear.

Here's what you've got to remember: Even if your lights get cut off, you can still see your vision. The vision is in your mind, not in this world and wasn't given to you by man; your vision was given to you by God. The lights are out, but your vision can be clearly seen. There can be noise all around you, but you can still hear your calling.

HOLD ON

FAILURE ENDURANCE

All the disappointments. All the failure. All the pain. All the setbacks. All the defeat. Your resources are gone. Your money is gone. Your friends and family can't help you, but this is what I've got to do! I've got to dig deep. I've got to internalize my vision, without internalizing my circumstances. I've got to get there. I'm beaten up. I'm bloody, but my head is unbowed. I'm down, but I'm not out.

But when you talk with someone you love, and they shut down, get gritty, and show you negativity seemingly out from nowhere, it's unexplainable. I get it! I know it hurts. But deal with the disappointment. Deal with the hurt that reminds you of your past failures. It's a setback. I get it! But it's not a defeat. Instead it is an opportunity to "become" your higher more authentic self.

Why? Because you're going to hold on to your dreams. Hold on to your fight. Hold on to your gravity. Hold on to your pushing. Hold on to your growing. Hold on to your learning. Hold on to your work.

Why? Because it's right here! It's in this space, and it's here where God reveals His grace. It's here where His grace becomes manifested. It's always right here. And that's when He steps in when you move out on faith rather than by what you see.

So what, you're in the dark about what is happening in this moment, yet your vision of God's promise remains clear.

Vision is not with your eyes; it's
in your heart, it's in your head.

Why? Because you still see it. Because the future is unclear, and you have begun to feel fear, but guess what you do? You move **toward** it. You embrace these failures, you embrace these disappointments, you embrace unknowns, you embrace these things that are beating you up. You don't run from them, you embrace them. Because in the moment you embrace them, right here, in the space is where God steps in, where God manifests His grace. It's been there all along.

But here's the thing: what you didn't recognize is what already happened, for it wasn't you that endured your failure. It wasn't you that shortened or lessened your endurance or strengthened your endurance. That wasn't you. That was not you, because you were afraid.

That was the you that God created you to be. That was the you that you stepped into when you got your vision. That was the you that you stepped into when you made a decision. That was the you that you became when you realized that it was not about you. It's about God. It was a God showing up. And what allowed God to show up? It's because you showed up. And when you show up, you don't show up as yourself, you show up as the next level of yourself, a higher iteration of yourself, and you show up as who He intended you to be. And who He intended you to be starts in your heart and your mind and your decision. It's your vision. It's internalized. Woe is unto me if I don't get there.

So, know that God's already there. You still see his vision and hear his calling. That's God.

That's the God in you. You thought it was you, only it wasn't. The version of you that showed up, wasn't the you that you're familiar with. It was the you that you can rely on. It was the you that looked for your shadow, because it's right there. It's right there in that space where you had nothing left. Then you looked for your shadow, by stepping into His light.

Suddenly resources you did not know you had begin to show up. Now that you still got a little bit of resources and you still got a little bit of endurance, you still got a little bit of energy, you still got a little bit of fight, that's when you're not going to give into your circumstances and failure is no longer an option. You know your shadow is there but you aren't looking for it. Like right now. Right now as you sit there reading this book, you're not looking for your shadow. I bet you it's somewhere real close. Stop. Look around, I bet if you put in some effort right now, that you find your shadow. I know you are not reading in the dark, and so you must be reading in the light and therefore your shadow is there, and if your shadow is there, the next level of you is also there.

Watch this. It's funny what happens when God shows up.

THE BLIND BEGGAR ASKS TO BE HEALED

There's a story in the Bible recorded in John 9 about a blind man. This man was born blind. In biblical times, it was believed that any person who was born with a disparity or disability or some type of shortcoming as in being blind for example that he or she is probably paying for the sins of the parents. We don't know what this man's story is. All we know is that he shows up in the bible and he is blind. This blind man was also a beggar and everybody in the city knows him as a beggar. They have seen him as a blind beggar his whole life. Everyone knows him. Everybody looks down at him. Everybody walks past him. You know how we sometimes do when we see people begging, panhandling and standing in the street, half dressed and we just don't want to be bothered.

So, he comes across Jesus and he asks Jesus to bless him with sight.

Jesus then spits on the ground. Then he took his spittle and made clay and places it upon the blind man's eyes.

Now, I struggled with this because we're talking about our Father. We're talking about the Creator of all things. We're talking about Jesus, who really didn't need to spit on the ground. He didn't need to make any clay. He didn't need dirt. Jesus could have just said, "You're healed," and it would have been done. He's Jesus. He didn't even have to say anything. He could have just thought it . . . thought it, and it would have been done. It would have been so ordered.

Jesus could have just snapped his finger and touched his eyes and sight could have been restored. One woman simply touched the hem of His garment and she was healed. Surely if she can touch the hem of a garment, you don't need to spit on the ground in the dirt and then place it on a blind man's face. And then, Jesus says, "Go and wash in the Pool of Siloam."

And Siloam in Hebrew means *sent*. S-E-N-T, sent. So, the man was sent. I have often times wondered, why would Jesus choose to handle this man this way and then why would Jesus then send this blind man on somewhere that he has never been knowing this man cannot see.

How many of us look at our circumstances as they are at any given moment, and ask ourselves why this happening to us, why we must endure so much more than seems fair. Why has this burden been thrust on me?

When we are talking about failure endurance. We're talking about how much more can you stand. How much had this guy already been through? He was born blind. In his story when we meet him for the first time he is in his late 30's and so we know he spent three decades blind. So he too, has been beaten up. Do you think his endurance might be weak? He is accustomed to being in the dark, yet we become afraid in the dark. He was a beggar. He was already in lack. Yet even in his lack, his faith and his courage made him ask to be healed with a spirit of expectancy. He asked in spite of his circumstances. Why would he even ask in light of what he had been through? What audacity to even ask. But he held on. He held onto his dreams. He held onto his fight. He held onto his gravity. He kept pushing, learning. Leaning. He kept working, begging, existing. He held on. He had some disappointments. He had some failures and setbacks. Might he have felt defeated, or do you think he had some pain, or do you think his resources were gone, or do you think his money was gone? Did he have any friends to stand by and help him? Who walked him get to the Pool of Siloam? Nobody. He was sent. He was sent by himself because he was alone. How many of you feel alone right now? How many of you are afraid because you're alone? You are neve alone.

If

By Rudyard Kipling

If you can keep your head when all about you

Are losing theirs and blaming it on you,

If you can trust yourself when all men doubt you,

But make allowance for their doubting too.

If you can wait and not be tired by waiting,

Or being lied about, don't deal in lies,

Or being hated, don't give way to hating,

And yet don't look too good, nor talk too wise:

If you can dream—and not make dreams your master;

If you can think—and not make thoughts your aim;

If you can meet with Triumph and Disaster,

And treat those two impostors just the same;

If you can bear to hear the truth you've spoken

Twisted by knaves to make a trap for fools,

Or watch the things you gave your life to, broken,

And stoop and build 'em up with worn-out tools:

If you can make a heap of all your winnings

And risk it on one turn of pitch-and-toss,

And lose, and start again at your beginnings

And never breathe a word about your loss;

If you can force your heart and nerve and sinew

To serve your turn long after they are gone,

And so hold on when there is nothing in you

Except the Will which says to them: "Hold on!"

If you can talk with crowds and keep your virtue,

Or walk with Kings—nor lose the common touch,

If neither foes nor loving friends can hurt you,

If all men count with you, but none too much;

If you can fill the unforgiving minute

With sixty seconds' worth of distance run,

Yours is the Earth and everything that's in it,

And—which is more—you'll be a Man, my son!

FAILURE ENDURANCE

NOTES

Chapter **5**

(6E x 10X) = Greatness

Greatness is more than a shadow, it is also a formula. Throughout this book, we've talked over and over about every little detail you need to go through, in order to step into that shadow, to find that greatness.

It's the vision that you have created. It's the thing that you've visualized, you've internalized, you've now strategized and decided you are going to implement, and you are going to overcome obstacles by any means necessary. It's your vision.

(6E x 10X) = GREATNESS

EXPECTANCY

Your vision must have a spirit of *expectancy*. Where does that come from? The expectation is the vision. What do you see for yourself?

EDUCATION

What is it that you need to know that's going to help you get there that you don't have? And how will it happen? What is it that you must learn that you don't currently know? What is your plan for creating an environment to learn and educate yourself? James Baldwin wrote that "people who cling to their delusions find it difficult, if not impossible, to learn anything worth learning: a people under the necessity of creating themselves must examine everything and soak up learning the way the roots of a tree soak up water." The Price of the Ticket: Collected Nonfiction 1948-1985, Page 516.

EXTRAPOLATION

Means to extract from, to withdraw from, to pull out of and then apply what it is you pull out. How will you extrapolate what you have read in this book to transform your life and walk in your purpose? What is the one thing that you know you most need to work on or the one concept, idea or theory that you know most applies to you and how will you work through that reality.

ELEVATION

Throughout Greatness is a Shadow, we have stressed the Greatness that comes when going to the Next Level. What or who are you becoming as part of your transformation? We're going to place ourselves at a higher level, a higher place. Why? Because we're not going to do the things we once did. We're not going to make the mistakes we once made. We're going to do more, be more, have more, because we're going to do it differently and with a spirit of expectancy created from a made-up mind and clear vision. Successful completion of one level logically follows to the next level.

EXECUTION

Where in your life are you going to begin to maneuver differently? Is it in your mind, body, being, balance, family, faith, finances, fitness? What is your strategy for execution? Who will you align yourself with, and what resources will you need to carry out your new expectant filled life?

Whatever you do, do not wait until you think you are ready or its finally time to begin execution. Tomorrow is not promised, nor should it be, because tomorrow does not exist. All we have is today. Greatness has a sense of urgency inextricably intertwined with it because, our Greatness has no bounds. Stop waiting for the right time. The time is now. Although you may honestly believe you are not ready or there are things not quite in place, just know that the next level in you must be called forth. Starting without everything you need forces you to raise your standards for yourself and go harder than you normally might to make up for what you do not have.

EXCELLENCE

With excellence, you've got greatness. The terms are somewhat synonymous. Greatness is a shadow. What is that thing, that one thing that you are going to do to take you to the next level? Excellence! That's what this whole book has been about. It's been about what's already in you, and it's been about getting it out of you. If you follow these six Es; *expectation, education, extrapolation, elevation* and *execution,* you will have **excellence**.

- Expectation
- Education
- Extrapolation
- Elevation
- Execution
- Excellence

To carry out the 6E, I encourage to do a written audit. Remember your vision must be clear, and how you plan to execute that vision must also be clear. One of the greatest roadblocks to Execution is not having a vision (Strategy) on how you will get there. The audits help you navigate the road blocks.

There are three audits.

Audit 1. You need to have an *honesty* audit.

Audit 2. You need to have a *resource* audit.

Audit 3. You need to have a *trust* audit.

AUDIT 1. THE HONESTY AUDIT

The honesty audit occurs when you look in the mirror and you ask yourself, honestly, where I am <u>not</u> doing my best? Where in my life is it that I wish I was doing better? Where in my life MUST I do better? Maybe there is one thing or maybe there are several things you want to purposefully, consciously and intentionally commit to. Decide what they are and jot them into your audit.

The peculiar thing about the honesty audit is that it does not even require you to be honest. You know why? Because the thing that you are asking yourself, you already know it. How do you know? Because it pains you. You think about it every day, you ignore it– every day, you hide from it, you bury it, you disguise it, you disguise yourself so it can't find you and you can't find it. The honesty part of it comes not in identifying what it is; it's more in acknowledging that there is something or things that you know exist where you know you need to do better.

The Honesty Audit means acknowledging that which you already know. You've got to be honest with yourself. Don't hide from it. Recognize it. Acknowledge it. Accept it. Now let's deal with it head on. Look at it. Touch it. Smell it. Despise it. Decide you want to change it.

The moment you can acknowledge it is the moment you're honest with yourself, and there's something transformative about that honestly.

STEP 2. THE RESOURCE AUDIT

The Resource Audit means figuring out what resources we have available to us to meet the challenge we know we need to face. The resource audit is how you will turn obstacles into opportunities and chaos into order. The resource audit forces you to look around at what you have and what you don't have and compare those resources to what you actually need. Whatever you don't have is overcome by resources or by resourcefulness. Many of us will lack the resources and assets to get where we need to be. None of us lack the resourcefulness to get what we need, if we want it bad enough. You must use your weaknesses as your creative strengths and recognize them within your audit.

Step 3. The Trust Audit

The last thing we're going to do is we're going to do a trust audit. A trust audit is where we will trust ourselves to continually reassess and measure our progress toward our goal. Here's what I know about you and I don't know you. I know that where you are right now is either where you want to be or it isn't. And if it isn't, we also know that all of the reasons point to you. They point to the decisions that you've made, the people that you've chosen to be in your life, the people that you've chosen not to be in your life. But you know what, don't beat yourself up over that. You did the best you could with the information you had. Maybe there were times when you looked at your available choices, but you made the wrong one anyway because it felt the best at that time. Don't beat yourself up over that because none of us are perfect.

Audits are necessary to maintain the integrity of your efforts. When looking at one's self, it can sometimes be hard to be objective. Certainly, you would never want to second guess all your decisions. Since many of your daily strategic tasks will be instinctive, intuitive and circumstantially prescribed, many people

(6E x 10X) = GREATNESS

find themselves in a "reactive" state of mind rather than a "proactive" state of mind. Proper, consistent use of the audits allows you to detach from the reactive nature of the decisions you have made, and now allows you to think more comprehensively regarding providence, foresight and intuition. Now, you can maneuver in such a way, where you are moving fluidly with the market or its conditions, and less urgent reactions to movements and developments in the marketplace.

This type of assessment and constant reassessment forces you to always be accountable. In addition, it provides direction ahead of occurrences rather than in response to occurrences. It is vitally important to always be nimble and capable of moving when necessary to capitalize on some new opportunity or avoid some unforeseen calamity.

CONCLUSION

With this knowledge, see something beyond where you are right now. Greatness is a Shadow has the power of transforming one's circumstances. You can choose to allow the principles in this book to either confine you or free you. You can be open to these ideas and principles or you can reject them.

Accordingly, if you see these concepts as meaningless, then choose to create your own reality where you create the life you deserve. You have greatness in you, so go out and live that greatness to the fullest.

On the other hand, if you see these concepts as transformative and applicable to your life, then I encourage you to embrace them with a fearless spirit and bold intentions. Claim your greatness and go get what is already yours. Cast your shadow and transform your life and live in your purpose.

Whatever you choose to allow for yourself is totally up to you. But choose. You can be as happy as you are, or you can be as happy as God wants you to be. Whatever you do, just remember the daily choices are up to you and that those choices matter more than you know. They may seem to only impact the current day, but the long-term implications of compounding effects must always be remembered.

There will always be the choice you make, the results you get, the excuse you had for what you chose and the blame you create on someone else for what you decided if it does not go as you hoped. Therefore, choose wisely.

As you have turned each page it is my hope that I have helped you realize that all of us have fears and all of us have so much to be thankful for. None of us should judge ourselves based on our successes nor our failures in our lives thus far. Know that everything that has

(6E x 10X) = GREATNESS

happened in your life was preparation for what the universe has in store for you. Live boldly and go hard. Have a spirit of expectancy and cast your shadow of Greatness.

BARRY M. JOHNSON

INSPIRE. EMPOWER. LEAD.

Barry M. Johnson serves the Heart, Purpose and Passion of the people.

PUBLIC SPEAKING

Barry ignites an enthusiastic, high-energy environment that produces measurable results. Your audience, participants and guests will gain insights and empowerment that will fuel innovation, creativity, leadership and participant inclusion.

THE BARRY M. JOHNSON PURPOSE

The purpose of The Barry M. Johnson Empowerment Group is to be the nation's leading "Influencer" & "Empowerment Training" firm.

THE BARRY M. JOHNSON APPROACH

Our approach is very specific and effective. Everything our organization does, we do with a spirit of excellence. We see your organization not only as our client, but our partner. Our "partnerships" are governed by three simple values: **Inspire. Empower. Lead.**

We INSPIRE: by (a) innovation, (b) vision and (c) real world application.

We EMPOWER: by (a) insight, (b) direction and (c) strategic solutions.

We LEAD: by (a) being purpose driven and (b) elevating the consciousness and commitment of our "client/partners" to impact change through their own organizational platforms.

CJ LEGACY PUBLISHING INC

BARRY M. JOHNSON
INSPIRE. EMPOWER. LEAD.

The Barry M. Johnson Empowerment Group was established to serve as the nation's leading "influencer" and "empowerment training" firm. I train and develop clients, groups, organizations and companies to become peak performers and influencers at every level.

My passion is helping others transform their lives and their businesses through my live "Elevation" events, books, public speaking engagements, mentoring and media appearances.

I've been blessed to work with people from every walk of life which has included current and future entrepreneurs to aspiring millennials, to top entertainment and sports celebrities, to some of the nation's leading corporate executives.

I coach people on reaching **PEAK PERFORMANCE** in leadership, negotiation, entrepreneurship, business strategy, digital marketing, public policy, real estate, brand development & crisis issues management and organizational turnarounds.

The Barry M. Johnson brand undertakes everything we do with a spirit of **EXCELLENCE**. If you want to learn more about any of these programs please visit my website: *www.BarryMJohnson.com*

Finally, you should know that I am passionate about giving back and service to those who are less fortunate. So, I am proud to announce that in 2017, you will see the launch of a non-profit organization that will serve the community at large in education, domestic violence and homelessness: **The H.O.P.E. Foundation, Inc.**

P: 470.891.3572 ◆ *E: Barry@BarryMJohnson.com* ◆ *W: www.BarryMJohnson.com*

OUR PROGRAMS:

Public Speaking ◆ Business Mastery ◆ Strategic Planning ◆ Diversity and Inclusion ◆ Millennial Insight
Team Building ◆ Business Coaching ◆ Mastermind Diamond Elite ◆ Power, Purpose, Passion Elite

Made in the USA
Columbia, SC
25 September 2018